SERIES EDITOR: LEE JOHNSON

OSPREY MILITARY MEN-AT-ARMS 312

THE ALGERIAN WAR 1954-1962

TEXT BY
MARTIN WINDROW

COLOUR PLATES BY
MIKE CHAPPELL

OSPREY
MILITARY

Filmset in Singapore by Pica Ltd.
Printed through World Print Ltd., Hong Kong

Editor: Sharon van der Merwe
Design: Alan Hamp @ Design for Books

For a catalogue of all books published by Osprey Military please write to:
OspreyMarketing, Reed Books, Michelin House, 81 Fulham Road,
London SW3 6RB

Author's Note

Consistent typography is hardly possible in a text scattered with
terms in both French and Arabic, many of the latter transliterated from
French sources. Generally I have only italicised Arabic words at their
first appearance and, for emphasis and clarity, a few French technical
and slang terms. I have not usually italicised French unit titles, etc.,
and have therefore used English capitalisation, e.g. Régiment de
Tirailleurs Algériens rather than the more correct *régiment de
tirailleurs algériens*.

Equally, I have not drawn fine distinctions between the Algerian FLN
(Front de Libération Nationale, the overall political organisation) and
the ALN (Armée de Libération Nationale, the military structure); generally I have used the latter when referring to any armed operations
except for urban terrorism.

Acknowledgements

I am extremely grateful for all assistance received during the prepa-
ration of this book and beforehand, particularly from Will Fowler, who
was as generous as always; from Jean-Luc Delauve, and Jim
Worden.

Publisher's Note

Readers may find it helpful to study this title in conjunction with the following
Osprey publications:
MAA 300 *French Foreign Legion since 1945*
Elite 6 *French Foreign Legion Paratroops*

Artist's Note

Readers may care to note that the original paintings from which the
colour plates in this book were prepared are available for private sale.
All reproduction copyright whatsoever is retained by the Publisher. All
enquiries should be addressed to:

14 Downlands, Walmer, Deal, Kent CT14 7XA

The publishers regret that they can enter into no correspondence
upon this matter.

THE ALGERIAN WAR
1954-1962

THE BACKGROUND

I T IS HARD, after 40 years, to convey the public impact of France's war to maintain her colonial grip on Algeria; yet in the late 1950s this ugly conflict dominated Europe's media to almost the same extent as would Vietnam ten years later.

It brought France to the verge of military *coup d'état*; it destroyed the Fourth Republic, and decisively transformed the French constitution. It destroyed thousands of careers; bitterly divided the French military and political classes for a generation; and sent hundreds of thousands of European settler families into often ruinous exile.

Its exact cost in lives is unknown. Some 25,000 French troops died in action, by accident or of disease; some 3,600 European civilians were killed or disappeared, and a similar number of loyal Muslim troops were killed. The Algerian guerrillas lost perhaps 155,000 killed outright, and many more died of wounds; Muslim civilian deaths from all causes easily exceeded 50,000 even before the vengeful post-ceasefire bloodbath, which killed anything up to twice as many. The much-quoted total estimate of a million Algerian dead is now discounted, but the true cost was certainly at least half that – a sufficiently monstrous figure.

Conventionally presented as just another successful mid-20th century colonial rebellion fought on the Maoist model, this war was in fact

The ruling image of the French Army in the Algerian War years: paratroopers parade in red berets and *'tenue leopard'*, with slung MAT49 sub-machine guns. This is the 1er BPC photographed at Port Fouad in December 1956.

shaped by its specific time and its particular antagonists; and it offers an interesting example of the military defeat of a revolutionary movement, which nevertheless gained its ultimate objective by political means. In a text of this length there is obviously space for only the most general summary of the military aspects, and none at all for the very complex political background; interested readers are recommended to Alistair Horne's classic *A Savage War of Peace* (see bibliography on p. 38).

The Algeria of the 1950s

By the early 1950s Algeria had enjoyed for nearly a century the official status of 'France overseas' – a constitutional fiction to which many Frenchmen clung passionately, ostensibly justified by the parliamentary representation in Paris of her three departments (from west to east, Oran, Algiers and Constantine, popularly called the Oranais, Algérois and Constantinois). However, only a tiny minority of the Muslim population held French citizenship rights or significant property. Since the initial French landings in 1830 on a coastline under the nominal authority of the decaying Ottoman Empire, a vast, unexploited, and more or less chaotic tribal hinterland had been transformed into France's largest colony: a source of cheap agricultural produce, and a captive market for French manufacturers.

The Muslim population had exploded to some eight million, at a time when France had a weak economy and runaway inflation. Some 75 per cent of Muslims were illiterate; they suffered chronic unem-

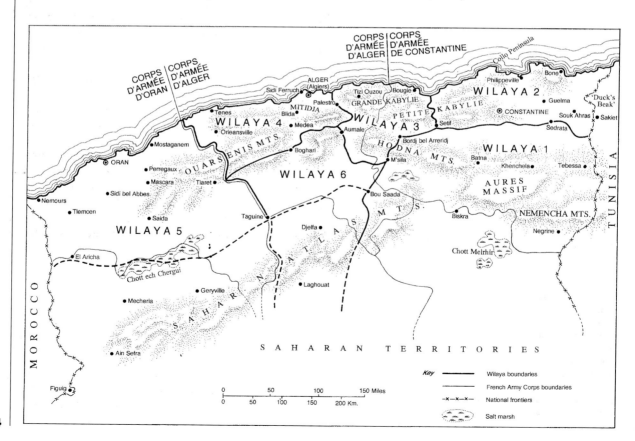

4

Early ALN volunteers pose with Mauser rifles and an automatic pistol; in November 1954 it is believed that the ALN had no more than 350 weapons, of which many were shotguns.

LEFT Sketch map of inhabited northern Algeria; the administrative boundaries were more or less theoretical when projected down into the Sahara. Most of this vast country is empty desert; its most southerly point – in 3 degrees E, 19 degrees N – lies some 1,200 miles south of Algiers. A few actions took place around the oases on the desert routes, e.g. Timimoun, approx. 230 miles further south than Ain Sefra. Note that only main mountain massifs are identified – apart from the Mitidja and other narrow coastal plains virtually the whole area of the map is mountainous.

ployment, poor health, and real hunger. The great majority of those who did have work were peasant farmers or urban labourers scraping a subsistence in more or less abject poverty.

Although outright-banditry was far from unknown in remote areas, few Muslims were involved in politically motivated subversion. Rural villagers accepted the authority of traditional community elders, whose obedience to the often distant French administration was rewarded by petty privileges. The older generation were often genuinely loyal to France, the *caids* (chieftains) and rural constables wearing their World War medals with pride; activists contemptuously dismissed this class as the *Beni Oui-Oui*, the 'Yes-Yes Tribe'. The urban poor were more restive; trade unions provided some focus of discontent, although the Communist Party was never strong. However, pressure for Muslim rights – either internal self-government, independence, or even complete integration with France – had long been building up among the small but significant academic and professional class which had benefited from French education.

Although the strains had become more mixed in the towns, an age-old suspicion persisted between the highland Berbers of the Aurès and Kabylia and the lowland Arabs. The Berbers were the poorer and more warlike of the two communities; but Algerians in general have been characterised by their own writers as tough, stoic, proud, stubborn, secretive, violently quarrelsome, and unforgiving – 'a people of right-angles, without curves'.

They were also given to extreme physical cruelty. Torture was commonplace; the knife – to cut throats, and to inflict appalling mutilations as a warning to others – was the weapon of choice (throat-cutting is associated with sheep-killing, and is thus a deliberately insulting death). Throughout the war many more Muslims died at the hands of their fellow Algerians than of the French.

The great majority of productive land, commerce and industry, and virtually all political and administrative power lay with the long-established 1.2 million-strong European settler community (known as *colons* or *pieds noirs*), mainly of Spanish, Italian, Corsican and Alsatian stock. Apart from a small liberal intelligentsia the *colons* were politically and racially conservative, their attitudes to the Muslims ranging from paternalism to callous bigotry. Although there were many *colons* and Muslims whose shared love for their often stunningly beautiful country brought them together in friendship, the twin walls of religion and racial injustice would always ultimately separate them.

Over the years various half-hearted attempts were made by Paris to reform Algerian local government in favour of Muslim advancement; grudging enough, these gestures were consistently undermined by the *colons*. The whites tended to be as volatile, headstrong, violent and unforgiving as the Muslims. They regarded France with the schizophrenic mixture of enthusiasm and resentment typical of all settler communities. They were rightly conscious that it was they who had built Algeria – draining the marshes, irrigating the wilderness, and bringing the fertile north, which enjoyed much the same climate and scenery as southern Europe, under widespread cultivation. They were fiercely determined to cling to what they had; and they saw betrayal in any hint of compromise from Paris.

Factional hostilities and conspiracies divided each of the three main parties to the war – French, *colons* and Muslims; but it was probably the dysfunctional relationship between Paris and the *colons* which destroyed any chance of a solution short of total victory and total defeat. France's constitutional arrangements under the Fourth Republic also made for a rapid succession of chronically weak and unstable governments, unable either to reach a settled view of the Algerian dilemma or to prosecute policy – any policy – effectively and consistently.

From 1958 a fourth party entered the equation, and came to dominate it: General Charles de Gaulle. The man who gave France back her self-respect in 1940-45 had retired from public life in 1946, disgusted by party politics; he retained a unique moral authority, and during the most squalid episodes of the Fourth Republic many Frenchmen's thoughts turned toward that huge, eloquent silence at Colombey-les-Deux-Églises. When summoned back to office in 1958 he understood that military success could not preserve the status quo. Publicly enigmatic while he consolidated his grip on power, he worked to create the conditions for some kind of negotiated peace which would preserve the future of the *colons,* as well as essential French interests, in a semi-independent Algeria. He would be defeated by a combination of *colon* intransigence; the FLN's determination not to be manoeuvred away from their goal of complete independence; and the absence of any credible, moderate intermediaries on either side after years of mutual murder. During the war extremists on both sides had targeted their more open-minded fellow countrymen, punishing any sign of compromise with savage atrocities and reprisals which gave the spiral of hatred another twist.

France's humiliation in 1940 had robbed her in Muslim eyes of much of her *baraka* – the spiritual force enjoyed by the strong and successful; and on VE Day in May 1945 celebration turned to horror around the Algerian town of Sétif. An anti-French Muslim demonstration got out of hand; panicky shots were fired; mobs ran amok, spreading out to butcher more than a

A French patrol in Kabylia; the northern slopes of the main mountain chains offered guerrillas thick cover, with cedar, scrub oak and cork forest, and dense undergrowth to shelter them from French aircraft. (Courtesy Jim Worden)

hundred European civilians; and over the weeks which followed French troops and European lynch-mobs killed at least 6,000 Muslims more or less at random – the true figures can never be known. The Sétif massacres were astonishingly little discussed in France, where Algerian unrest was complacently dismissed as apolitical banditry. French public attention was soon focused on Indochina, the arena for the first great post-war challenge to France's colonial authority. Among the Muslims, however, Sétif was a turning point, discrediting moderate voices and acting as a recruiting sergeant for outright revolution.

Large numbers of Muslim troops served with the French Expeditionary Corps in Indochina between 1946 and 1954; although generally brave and loyal, some were inevitably attracted by the Viet Minh's anti-colonial propaganda. Eventually the French Army was defeated once again, and this time by her own colonial subjects; the fall of Dien Bien Phu in May 1954 brought her to the negotiating table to agree a rapid retreat from South-East Asia.

During the early 1950s there had been growing unrest in France's other two North African territories. Morocco and Tunisia were not outright colonies, but protectorates over which French rights were limited by international agreement, and their clamour for independence had to be addressed. In 1952-56 French forces were deployed on security operations in both countries, being drawn from Algeria in 1952-54 and thereafter from units returning from Indochina. France also had a major commitment to her sector of the Iron Curtain across

Landscape with infantry: the wilderness of the eastern Constantinois, where French intervention units spent much of their war 'nomadising'. (Courtesy Jim Worden)

Germany, where the best-equipped units of her conscript army faced the Soviet threat. Since the 1940s the French army in Algeria had also been committed to providing training, replacement, and transit facilities for Indochina, where large numbers of professional troops (as opposed to conscripted short-term national servicemen) remained well into 1955.

Although there were more than 60,000 troops in Algeria when the first shots of the war were fired on the night of 1 November 1954, potentially effective manpower was thus limited to some 17,000, of whom two-thirds were Muslim Tirailleurs and Spahis; immediately available combat troops numbered some 3,500. Prior warnings of forthcoming trouble had been ignored by the generally inert military authorities.

SUMMARY OF MAIN EVENTS

November 1954–1956

1954: Nov: The first co-ordinated ALN attacks on public installations, military and police posts in Aurès and Kabylia to capture arms have variable success. Call for general rising largely dismissed by French, who respond to 'banditry' by major punitive sweeps, **Nov.-Jan**; some success, but survival of guerrillas gives them prestige in Muslim eyes, and indiscriminate repression (including some air and artillery bombardment of villages, mass round-ups and ill-treatment) increases FLN support.

1955: Feb: Governor-General Soustelle begins liberal reforms and a welfare programme, which is countered from the **spring** by rapidly spreading ALN terrorism against Muslim 'collaborators', European farms, and rural schools – i.e. the *colon* economy, and any focus of Muslim/European co-operation – throughout Constantinois. ALN assembles 50-man companies to ambush troops, **April-May:** FLN gain Third World recognition at Bandung Conference. To hit *colon* agriculture, all Muslims are ordered to give up smoking and alcohol, on pain of mutilation and death. The French institute a policy of 'collective responsibility' against the population, with predictable results. **June:** ALN regional commander Zighout declares unlimited terror campaign against European and Muslim civilians, later backed by FLN ideological chief Ramdane Abane. **Aug.:** Grisly ALN massacre of 120 civilians at Philippeville outrages public opinion; army and *colon* reprisals kill several thousand Muslims. Setback for reformists seeking to remove root causes of unrest; escalating

Suspect being searched by men of the 9e Zouaves, winter 1954-55; at this early date they wear fully badged M1946 wool battledress.

cycle of atrocity, reprisal, and consequent increased FLN support. Paris announces recall of 60,000 reservists. Armed clashes, and ALN grip on the population, both increase country-wide.

1956: Jan-Feb: Soustelle recalled. *Colon* riots force Premier Mollet to rescind unpopular appointment of Gen. Catroux – Algiers mob discovers its power over Paris. **March: Morocco and Tunis achieve independence**, French garrisons leave all but small enclave in Tunisia.

ALN thereafter acquire training camps and logistic bases in both countries, planning to use these over-border bases to support eventual escalation to mobile phase of revolutionary war by building conventional manoeuvre units. However, continuing Moroccan and Tunisian vulnerability vis-à-vis France limits permitted ALN activities throughout war.

May: 20 conscripts of 9e RIC killed by Ali Khodja's ALN unit near Palestro – first major conscript casualties; public outrage encourages French hard line. **30 Sep.:** FLN urban bombing campaign against civilian targets opens in Algiers; European casualties, and lynch-mob reprisals, will mount during winter. **22 Oct:** FLN external leaders including Ben Bella hijacked from Moroccan airliner, imprisoned by French. Anger in Morocco and Tunisia leads to increased help for FLN; removal of external leaders helps unify internal leadership. **Nov:** Anglo-French landings in Suez Canal Zone, Egypt. President Nasser subsequently increases aid to FLN, who step up drive for international recognition, profiting from French unpopularity; Suez climb-down increases French Army's contempt for political authorities.

1957–Summer 1958

1957: Jan-Mar & May-Sept.: Gen. Massu's 10e DP given free hand against urban FLN bombers and assassins in **'Battle of Algiers'**.

Paras control casbah by massive ID checks and enforced 'pyramid' structure of answerability by household, building, street and block representatives. Masked informers help screen Muslims picked up in mass sweeps; suspects interrogated under torture; many deaths in captivity, including FLN leader Lahbi Ben M'hidi. FLN networks in city steadily destroyed; others penetrated by French intelligence, and fleeing survivors will compromise rural Wilayas. ALN morale and recruiting slump.

Spring: Army effectiveness and morale improve; Sections Administratives Specialisées (SAS) 'hearts & minds' programme shows results, ALN defections increase. Gen. Beaufré, commanding ZEC, simultaneously applies population resettlement, psy-ops, ruthless hunting out of FLN politico-administrative infrastructure, 'free fire' operations against ALN bands; ALN forced onto defensive. **May:** Massacre of 300 villagers at Melouza, Kabylia, by Wilaya 3 leader Amirouche hands French propaganda coup. **July:** Si Chérif of Wilaya 6 defects to French with 330 men. **Sept.:** Algiers FLN chief Yacef Saadi captured; urban terrorism virtually halted. French complete **'Morice Line'** of Tunisian frontier defences. These seal off internal ALN from external forces and supplies:

ALN training with Lewis LMG; before 1957 automatic weapons were in very short supply. After Suez, Nasser provided about 500 Bren LMGs and 5,000 British rifles. Most other weapons had to be purchased for cash on the international market; the French secret services waged a lethal underground war to discourage the ALN's commercial suppliers.

460km of 5,000-volt electrified fence, barbed wire, minefields, with radar surveillance and constant ground and air patrols, guarded by 12,900 men. Similar defences soon completed on 720km of Moroccan frontier, with 9,500 men.

Dec: Gen. Salan appointed C-in-C. FLN/ALN leadership crisis; liquidation of brilliant political chief Ramdane Abane.

1958: Jan-July: 'Battle of the Frontiers': determined ALN attempts to bring in arms and troops from Tunisia lead to fiercest battles of war with French units in cleared strip extending one day's march inside frontier, particularly in 'Duck's Beak' sector near Guelma.

Jan: Amirouche launches destructive purge of Wilaya 3. **Feb:** Cross-border provocations prompt French bombing of Sakiet, Tunisia; international protests aid FLN's diplomatic campaign; but ALN monthly casualties on frontiers total 3,400 dead, 529 captured, and inside Kabylia (27 Jan-20 Feb), another 2,151 and 333. Total French casualties for month: 360 dead, 700 wounded. **March:** ALN monthly casualties on frontiers 3,132 dead, 715 captured. **April:** France without government for 37 days from 15th; crisis of authority in Algeria. ALN monthly casualties on frontiers 3,728 dead, 756 captured. **28 April-3 May:** Largest engagements of war near **Souk-Ahras.**

At least eight companies totalling *c.*1,300 men of ALN 2e & 4e Faileks (battalions) attempt to force Morice Line north and south of Souk-Ahras to reinforce Wilayas 2 and 3; some 800 succeed in crossing (mostly by digging under obstacles). Of these, 436 killed, 100 captured in first two days, another 93 killed later, by 9e, 14e & 18e RCP, 1er & 2e REP and motorised infantry; only approximately 160 escape into the interior; around 412 individual weapons and 46 machine-guns, one mortar and four bazookas are captured. French casualties over six days are 38 killed, and 35 wounded (many in 3e Cie./9e RCP).

13 May: A European mob seizes Algiers public buildings, and demands the

Legion motorised infantry pose with prisoners and recovered weapons: mostly Mauser K98 rifles, with pistols, a MAT49 and an MP40.

return to power of Gen. de Gaulle (French politico-military factions have been conspiring to same end). **June: De Gaulle becomes French Premier**; visits Algeria to great acclaim, and makes reassuring but ambiguous speech. **26 June:** Last major frontier battle near Tebessa: 300-strong ALN force retreats after losing 46 dead, 64 captured, these figures indicating loss of ALN morale. **July:** French estimate total ALN casualties Jan.-July at 23,534 dead and captured. ALN/FLN rift in face of defeats and purges; ALN abandon hope of reinforcing internal forces in significant strength.

September 1958-December 1959

Sept: FLN form provisional government in exile (GPRA), securing increased Arab League and Communist aid. De Gaulle's constitutional reforms massively supported in referendum; hopes rise of compromise peace. **Oct:** De Gaulle offers 'Peace of the Brave' – an amnesty for surrendering insurgents, safe-conduct for FLN to negotiate cease-fire; sufficient response to worry both FLN leaders and *colon*/army hard-liners. Judicial executions halted, release of detainees begun (*c.*13,000 Nov. 58-July 59). **Dec:** De Gaulle becomes President of France. Gen. Maurice Challe replaces Salan as C-in-C in Algeria.

1959: Feb-April: Operations against Wilaya 5 in the Oranais launch **'Challe Plan' offensive.**

Beginning in this relatively easier region, all available sector and intervention troops are committed, area by area, to the elimination of ALN and infrastructure. Sector and motorised troops concentrate in deep cordons; *commandos de chasse* track ALN units inside cordon until fixed by air and air-inserted observers; para and Legion intervention units and tactical air support concentrate, remaining in contact until enemy is destroyed; local FLN administration is rooted out; reserve units only move on when sector troops capable of dominating area permanently. **Apr-June:** Operation 'Courroie' against Wilaya 4 in the Algérois, eastern Ouarsenis. **July:** Operation 'Etincelles' in the Hodna Mountains to isolate Wilaya 3. **July-Oct.:** Operation 'Jumelles' against Wilaya 3 in Kabylia. **Sept.-Nov.:** Operation 'Pierres Precieuses' in ZNC, ZEC. Major losses and damage to ALN strength, support network, command structure, and morale; internal ALN ordered to disperse into section-sized units only; military activity henceforward largely reduced to low-risk sabotage and terrorism.

16 Sept.: De Gaulle publicly recognises prospect of Algerian 'self-determination', hoping military stalemate will persuade FLN to negotiate. Scenting French political weakness, they remain aloof – but the offer further angers *colon*/army conservatives.

1960 – April 1961

1960: 24-29 Jan. 'Barricades Week'. Europeans revolt in Algiers, fire on police; paras brought in, but refuse to confront *colons*. De Gaulle defuses

Legion paras, identified by the green berets which they always wore in preference to the Bigeard cap of the RCPs and RPCs, cross a watercourse (*oued*) during a summer sweep in typical Aurès terrain. Veterans tend to remember the heat, cold, grinding physical exhaustion and lack of sleep as vividly as their clashes with the ALN. (Courtesy Jim Worden)

crisis with broadcast speech, but obvious French disunity encourages the FLN to play a waiting game. Boumedienne, new ALN chief-of-staff, orders internal forces to mark time while he builds up external army as eventual bargaining counter; improves relations with Communist bloc, thus increasing pressure on France by prospect of direct Russian or Chinese intervention.

April: Operation 'Trident' in Aurès completes Challe Plan. **June:** De Gaulle publicly invites negotiation, but secret FLN/French peace talks at Melun fail. Terrorism continues, particularly targeting Muslims attracted by De Gaulle's offers; ALN infrastructure is quietly rebuilt. French electorate's war-weariness, and foreign criticism, both increase. **Nov.:** De Gaulle speech refers for first time to possible future 'Algerian Algeria'; European hard-line 'ultras' plan coup. **20 Dec.:** UN recognises Algerian right to self-determination.

1961: Jan: First assassinations by OAS (Secret Army Organisation) – *colon* 'ultras' and army deserters – in name of preserving *'Algérie francaise'*. **20-26 April:** Coup d'état in Algiers – **'Generals' Putsch'** – led by retired generals Salan, Challe, Zeller, and Jouhaud with some para units, in name of preserving French Algeria; fears of airborne attack on Paris. Coup fails when De Gaulle broadcasts appeal for loyalty to conscripts; implicated para units are disbanded; Challe surrenders, many officers arrested; others, led by Salan, go underground to continue futile but lethal OAS terrorism in Algeria and France.

May 1961-July 1962

May: Major OAS bombings begin in Algiers. FLN/French peace talks open at Evian. De Gaulle orders army to cease offensive operations.

Lt.Col. Jeanpierre leads his paras of the 1er REP through Algiers city, 1957. This admission that the Gendarmerie and the civil authorities had completely lost control, and that only *de facto* martial law offered a solution, was a turning-point in the French approach to the rebellion.

FLN do not reciprocate, stepping up operations sharply; with loss of initiative French casualties increase greatly over the following year. **July:** First Evian peace talks fail. **8 Sept:** Most violent of many OAS attempts on De Gaulle's life.

1962: Feb: More than 550 deaths in various OAS outrages finally destroy any significant French public support for *colon* cause. **7-19 March:** Second Evian peace talks; **cease-fire agreement signed between French and FLN. 20 April:** Salan captured. **June:** OAS/FLN truce. **3 July: France recognises Algerian independence**.

Ben Bella becomes first president of independent Algeria. French army withdraws except for temporary enclaves at Reggane in Sahara and Mers-el-Kébir

'The Battle of Algiers', 1957: paratroopers supervise a mass arrest in the casbah – where many tens of thoudands of Muslims inhabited a kilometre-square maze of interconnecting houses, courtyards, stairways, alleys and rooftops. Initial screening aided by local informers will suggest possible FLN supporters; rigorous interrogation, routinely involving torture by electrodes, will identify suspects, and help fill in intelligence officers' 'organigrams' of terrorist cells and hideouts. Targeted raids will follow, netting further prisoners for interrogation, bomb caches, and documents.

port. **June-July:** Enforced exodus of *c.*1,450,000 European *colons*, given choice between 'the suitcase and the coffin'. Only about 15,000 loyal *harkis* are resettled in France; abandoned, by the French between 50,000 and 100,000 Muslim men, women and children are butchered thereafter by the FLN, often with grotesque cruelty.

THE ARMY OF NATIONAL LIBERATION

Command Structure

The call for general insurrection in November 1954 was issued in the name of the National Liberation Front (FLN), a movement which had evolved from an 'alphabet soup' of previous nationalist factions. The external leadership was initially based in Cairo under Ahmed Ben Bella, and later in Tunis. Internal regional leaders were Lahbi Ben M'Hidi (Oran), Rabah Bitat (Algiers), Belkacem Krim (Kabylia), Mourad Didouche (north Constantine) and Mustafa Ben Boulaid (Aurès). Of the original nine most senior leaders only Krim would still be alive and at large after March 1957.

The FLN was divided into autonomous politico-military commands, *Wilayas*, each wholly responsible for regional activities: indoctrinating, mobilising, and taxing the civil population, by persuasion or terror; and recruiting, training, arming, and commanding the ALN. This

Yacef Saadi, the resourceful young leader of 1,400 FLN in the Algiers casbah. Cornered by the 1er REP on 24 September 1957 as his network was finally smashed, he demanded and received POW status from the French. The co-producer of Pontecorvo's classic (and remarkably even-handed) 1965 film *La Battaglia di Algeri*, in which he acted himself, he survived the post-independence chaos to become a successful businessman.

decentralised command, and widely differing local conditions, explain the unco-ordinated nature of operations for much of the war. The heart of the rebellion was always the remote highlands of the Aurès and Kabylia, whose mountains, canyons, hidden valleys, caves and cliff villages offered limitless hide-outs, and whose ALN leaders were inheritors of a tradition of blood-feud and banditry not unlike that of the North-West Frontier of India. Although he looked, in a suit, like a flabby small-town functionary, Belkacem Krim had in fact taken to the hills with a Sten gun as early as 1947; Ben Boulaid was a highly-decorated veteran of the Italian campaign; and Omar Ouamrane's military background was so respected that even as an ALN colonel he was always known as 'Sergeant' Ouamrane.

The Wilayas, and some prominent commanders and senior officers, were as follows (almost all used aliases):

Wilaya 1 (Aurès): Mustafa Ben Boulaid, Mahmoud Chérif, Hadj Lakhdar, Mohammed Amouri.

Wilaya 2 (N.Constantinois): Mourad Didouche, Youssef Zighout, Lakhdar Ben Tobbal, Ali Kafi.

Wilaya 3 (Kabylia; and sometimes embraced command of Algiers city): Belkacem Krim, Omar Ouamrane, Mohammedi Said, Col. Amirouche, Mohand Ou El-Hadj.

Wilaya 4 (Algérois): Rabah Bitat, Omar Ouamrane, Si Sadek, Si Lakhdar, Ali Khodja, Si Azzedine, Si M'hamed, Si Salah.

Wilaya 5 (Oranais): Lahbi Ben M'Hidi, Abdelhafid Boussouf, Houari Boumedienne, Col. Lotfi.

Wilaya 6 (Sahara and environs): Taieb El-Djoghali, Si Haouès.

The character and fortunes of the Wilayas varied dramatically at different times, as did the quality of leadership. Some commanders were outstanding; others were little more than feuding bandit chiefs. Even within the Arab and Berber communities local tribal differences and mutual suspicion persisted. A marked national characteristic was an instinctive suspicion of the cult of the individual. These factors, together with the sheer difficulty of command liaison, hampered operational effectiveness. Merciless warfare between various Muslim groups was pursued simultaneously with the war against the French, particularly between the FLN and the rival MNA nationalist movement (a tendency often exploited with great success by French intelligence agencies).

The 'general staff' (Co-ordinating and Executive Committee, CCE – which fled Algiers for Tunis in spring 1957) tightened up the command structure in early 1958, creating Western and Eastern staffs (COMs) in Morocco (for Wilayas 4, 5 and 6) and Tunisia (for Wilayas 1, 2 and 3) respectively. In January 1960 existing realities were recognised by the confirmation of Col. Houari Boumedienne – whose powerbase was the army-in-waiting in Tunisia – as chief-of-staff of the whole ALN.

Organisation and Equipment

The Soummam Conference of August 1956 established ALN tactical organisation: ranks from private (*djoundi*) to colonel (*sagh ettani*); the 11-man section (*faoudj*), 110-man company (*katiba*), and 350-man battalion (*failek*). In practice the shortage of arms, and French surveillance, nearly always limited units inside Algeria to katiba size.

An apparently deserted Berber *douar* in the hills, one of hundreds whose inhabitants were forcibly removed. By mid-1958 some 485,000 civilians had been resettled, and 100,000 more had fled into Tunisia and Morocco. In the short term this policy robbed the ALN of food, shelter and local guides, and created free-fire zones up to 30 miles wide inside the frontiers.

Katibas were numbered, beginning with that of the Wilaya (e.g. Katiba 533 was a unit of Wilaya 5). By May 1956 Si Lakhdar and Ali Khodja of Wilaya 4 had already formed the first Zonal Commando (Cdo.41). About 100 strong in five 20-man platoons, these commandos were a response to the ALN's patchy strength and equipment, concentrating the best available men and weapons for special training and missions.

The uneven flow of arms always dictated strength and level of activity. Desperately meagre in 1955, this improved sharply during 1956. French naval and espionage successes sometimes interrupted supplies, but it was the virtual sealing of the Tunisian and Moroccan frontiers in 1958 which left the Wilayas in critical straits from that summer until May 1961. Brief notes on specific ALN weaponry will be found in the Plates commentaries and captions. Generally speaking, after 1956 most regular field units were adequately armed with World War II rifles, SMGs, LMGs and grenades; there was a shortage of heavy machine guns and mortars; specialist weapons such as bazookas were always desperately rare; and apart from occasional harassing fire from mortars, artillery and AAA inside Tunisia, the French faced nothing heavier. Radios and medical resources were always in short supply, with the inevitable consequences for command and co-ordination, morale and numbers.

Strength and Morale

A detailed breakdown of ALN strength at any particular time is difficult, since both sides manipulated for propaganda purposes the distinction between full-time armed fighters (*moudjahiddine*), part-time guerrillas (*moussebiline*) and auxiliaries, and between fighters active inside Algeria and the 'Army of the Frontiers' waiting in Tunisia and Morocco. The core force in November 1954 was perhaps 500 armed men and 1,200 auxiliaries. Initial losses in winter 1954-55 may have reduced active fighters to as few as 350; but resentment at heavy-handed French repression, and the rapid spread of the FLN's grip over the population from 1955 hugely increased recruitment.

Recruits who could not be armed at once served initially as auxiliaries on intelligence, courier, and logistic duties. After the establishment of the external camps they were taken over the frontiers as soon as possible for training and equipment in Tunisia or Morocco. In late 1957 it is claimed that a monthly average of 1,000 armed men were passing back into Algeria. The sealing of the frontiers in 1958 prevented outwards as well as inwards movement, and noticeably reduced the quality of the internal forces.

Various quoted totals suggest that between early 1956 and early 1958 the internal strength was between 15,000 and 20,000 'regulars', plus at

A paratrooper directs an old Berber woman during the relocation of villagers from near Batna. Conditions in the resettlement camps varied between the grim and the tolerable; but all those forced off their ancestral land deeply resented being uprooted, and in the long term the policy increased FLN support. (Courtesy Jim Worden)

least the same number of part-time guerrillas; and that by January 1958 another 15,000 were under arms in Tunisia and Morocco. By January 1959 the regulars in Algeria had been reduced to some 8,000, but the Army of the Frontiers had rebuilt itself to 15,000 after the losses of spring 1958. In February 1960, 8,000 regulars are still claimed in Algeria despite the cost of the Challe offensives, but only 10,000 total in Tunisia and Morocco. Between December 1960 and August 1961 internal strength seems not to have grown, but the Army of the Frontiers was built up to some 25,000. By March 1962 Boumedienne had increased this to c.35,000 and was receiving Soviet bloc weapons including a little armour and artillery.

Since the Battle of the Frontiers, January-July 1958, was claimed to have cost the ALN c.23,500 dead, and Challe's 1959 operations a similar number, then if these totals are even approximately correct they suggest that recruitment among external refugees more than kept up with casualties, but that the replacements could not be moved into Algeria in any numbers after 1959.

ALN discipline, marrying revolutionary harshness with Islamic puritanism, was extremely severe. Conditions in the field were harsh; shelter, food and medical supplies were rudimentary; and despite local victories the odds were heavily against the ALN in most engagements with French intervention units from 1957. Morale was naturally volatile; in 1956 defections to the French were minimal, but after the frontier battles of 1958 they were running at 300 a month, and some units reportedly refused orders to attempt to cross. It was a tribute to their toughness and motivation that even when dispersed and forced back onto the defensive the hard core of fighters endured until the tide turned once more; and as soon as the French ceased offensive operations in May 1961 the ALN demonstrated remarkable powers of recovery.

Nevertheless, recruitment by kidnapping was common, and the resentment this caused accounted for many of the steady trickle of desertions back to the French. Before 1959 the *djounoud* were well aware of their likely fate if captured. If their surrender was even accepted, France refused to treat what were termed 'outlaws' as prisoners of war, and many were guillotined. However, the 'Peace of the Brave' offer of October 1958 tempted many to change sides to the *harkis* and *commandos de chasse*; the proportion of surrendered to killed increased from 27% in 1958 to 42% in 1959.

Whole ALN commands could turn rotten – or could be actively persuaded to rot, by the 2e Bureau and the 'dirty tricks' unit 11e Bataillon de Choc. Wilaya 3 was deeply penetrated by French intelligence in 1957, and its leader Amirouche ruined his command in 1958-59 by his obsessive witchhunt for traitors, torturing and killing thousands.

In early 1957 Wilaya 4's military chief Si Lakhdar led probably the most impressive of all ALN commands, and its political chief Si M'hamed was implanting a strong and democratic cell structure in the Algérois. In early 1958 they astutely neutralised a French intelligence attempt to establish a local Muslim counter-guerrilla force. Yet by summer 1959 – infected by Wilaya 3 – this command was tearing itself apart in bloody purges; and in June 1960 its leader Si Salah secretly flew to Paris to negotiate peace with De Gaulle. (Nothing came of this, and Si Salah was executed by the FLN.) This episode was caused partly by a rift between the beleaguered Wilaya commanders and the external provisional government; relations between the internal and external leadership were always difficult, and sometimes murderous.

THE FRENCH ARMY IN ALGERIA

By early 1955 the garrison had increased to some 74,000; reinforcements that spring brought the total to about 105,000 in July. About 60,000 reservists were recalled from summer 1955, bringing the garrison to approximately 200,000 by early 1956; during that year some 150,000 reservists were recalled, and military service for conscripts was increased to 27 months. The strength of *c.*400,000 reached by the end of 1956 would be maintained until 1962.

The essential characteristic of the garrison was its division into two distinct entities. The 'sector' or static troops, almost entirely conscripts and reservists, were dispersed over this immense country in an attempt to provide local security; while the General Reserve of airborne and motorised 'intervention' units, also largely conscripted but with an armature of volunteers and long-service professionals, acted as mobile fire-brigades.

The swampy Collo peninsula on the north-east coast was a notorious ALN refuge; these Legion paras are forced to wade during a sweep through thick cover. (Courtesy Jim Worden)

Divisional Organisation

Algeria, France's 10th Military Region, was divided into three Corps commands – the Corps d'Armée d'Oran, d'Alger, de Constantine; and the Saharan region, which had always been under military government. Each Corps area was divided into operational zones. For administrative and garrison purposes each zone was the fief of one or more light ('Voltigeur') Divisions each of *c.*8,600 men. Those deployed in mid-1956 were:
C d'A d'Oran: 12e, 13e & 29e DI, 5e DB (armoured)
C d'A d'Alger: 9e, 20e & 27e DI

ABOVE **Tanks, such as this M24 Chaffee of a Spahi regiment, were useful as mobile fire support in the cordons of all-arms operations, and played their part in 'ploughing' the cleared zones along the frontier barrages, but were impractical in the mountains where the intervention units spent much of their war. (Courtesy Jim Worden)**

C d'A de Constantine: 2e DIMot, 14e & 19e DI, 25e DIAP.

Reserve: 7e DIMot, 10e DP. Later the 4e DIMot, 11e & 21e DI would be deployed; and the 25e Aéroportée would become a full Parachute Division.

For example: in early 1957 the Corps d'Armée d'Oran comprised the Zone Nord Oranais (ZNO) with elements of the 4e Division d'Infanterie Motorisée – nine infantry battalions, one armoured cavalry regiment, one artillery group; Zone Centre Oranais (ZCO), with the 13e & 29e Divisions d'Infanterie – 15 infantry, 2 armoured, three artillery units; Zone Ouest Oranais (ZOO), 5e Division Blindée & 12e Division d'Infanterie – 26 infantry, three armoured, two artillery units; and Zone Sud Oranais (ZSO), with the rest of the 4e DIM – four infantry, three artillery units. Each zone also had various temporary irregular units, locally raised.

The proportion of career soldiers in the cadres of these formations was usually only about 15%, although in 1956 some 25% of the 29e DI's cadre and 5% of its troops were professionals.

The Sector Troops

The disadvantage of the sharp distinction between sector and intervention units was that the former were starved of all the human and material resources enjoyed by the latter, suffering particularly from a shortage of experienced junior officers and NCOs. The rapid expansion of 1955-56 strained France's ability to train, equip and officer these troops. Many reservists reported for duty only under protest; and discipline, morale and efficiency were not aided by the deployment of poorly prepared units of all types – cavalry, artillery, even logistics battalions – in the infantry role.

The great majority were committed to the policy of '*quadrillage*' – 'squaring', referring to map squares – which tied down huge numbers of men in only patchily successful attempts to protect European farms, Muslim villages, roads, railways, pylons, pipelines, and every other kind of target from attack or sabotage. Systematic *quadrillage* began in the northern Constantinois in June 1955 and became universal from July 1956.

Serving out their two dreary years in individual companies and platoons in often lonely and utterly comfortless posts scattered across the vast interior, most sector troops had no chance to build proper unit cohesion or operational skills. During long periods of numbing routine their only contact with the outside world might be the monthly resupply convoy, or mailbags dropped from a passing aircraft. Public preoccupation with the triumphs of *les paras* was bad for morale; the sector troops knew that they were second-class soldiers, but most were denied the opportunity to become anything else. Their only stimulus to efficiency was fear of the lurking enemy.

To young Frenchmen set down in this often beautiful but alien world, the Muslims' wretched poverty was depressing; their too-frequent casual ill-treatment by the authorities was shaming; and the exemplary atrocities inflicted on them by the FLN were horrifying. While few army posts stood in any serious danger of actual assault, the conscripts would hear frequent reports of ambushed convoys and patrols, mutilated casualties, and even occasional French prisoners dragged off to God knew what fate. Given their recognition of their own limitations, these stories did not improve confidence or initiative when ill-equipped conscripts were led out on patrols or night ambushes in active areas (one reads – admittedly extreme – accounts of platoons sent out with one round per rifle, three rounds per SMG, and one magazine for the LMG).

Against this general background there were, of course, impressive exceptions. Not all conscripts were banished to the '*bled* and the *djebel*' (the desert and the mountain). Those posted in areas such as the northern Oranais, with its large *colon* population, led a better life; occasional access to beaches, cafés and suntanned girls did wonders for

ABOVE **ALN fighter wearing US M1943 field jacket; his US web equipment includes suspenders and two rifle ammunition belts.** (Courtesy Will Fowler)

LEFT **Probably photographed in Tunisia at about the time of the Battle of the Frontiers, 1957-58, these clean, well-equipped ALN *djounoud* are still armed with old 1886 Lebel rifles, though note the central soldier with a German MP40, and a left shoulder patch – presumably an NCO.**

Women ALN volunteers examine a Luger pistol; note the openwork '*boule*-basket' carriers holding British grenades. The place of women in the movement was controversial: their theoretical 'revolutionary equality' was at odds with deeply felt Muslim prejudices. Although many suffered and died for the cause, women's emancipation quickly lost impetus after the cease-fire.

motivation. Long traditions and good leadership allowed cultivation of higher morale in some units – e.g. the Zouaves, with many local *colon* recruits. Some units were motorised with American trucks and half-tracks, and relatively better equipped for more pro-active mobile missions (e.g. the 26e, 60e, 151e, 152e and 153e RI facing the Morice Line).

Muslim and Mixed Units

Some 20,000 Muslim career regulars and another 20,000 conscripts served in Algeria in Tirailleur infantry regiments and autonomous battalions (RTA, BTA), and Spahi mechanised cavalry regiments (RSA); the 'Algérien' suffix was discontinued in 1958 following Moroccan and Tunisian independence. Initially these units had mixed French and Muslim cadres and Muslim troops.

A French source adds these units to peak figures of c.60,000 *harkis*, 20,000 *moghaznis* and 15,000 *commandos*; and lists some 9,000 desertions from the grand total. As 1956 – well before the numbers of such irregulars reached those levels – was the worst year, with 1,700 defections, it follows that there were many desertions from the regular units. Some involved groups of men shooting their leaders before taking their weapons over to the ALN. Equally, there were countless examples of courage and loyalty – the more impressive given the peril facing loyalists' families. Units still serving in Algeria in mid-1960 were:

Oran: 21e RT (ZNO); 2e RT, 2e & 14e BT, 2e & 23e RS (ZSO); 29e RT, 9e RS (ZEO).

Algiers: 1er BT (ZNA); 1er & 4e RT, 5e & 17e BT (ZSA); 9e BT, 5e RS (ZOA).

Constantine: 22e RT, 21e RS (ZNC); 7e RT (ZSC); 1er & 8e RS (ZNEC); 3e RT, 11e & 14e BT, 6e RS (ZOC).

From 1956 a new policy led to mixing of the races within units. By 1959 Tirailleur units would approach half Muslim, half *colon* composition; and most Metropolitan and Colonial units would also take in up to 25% Muslim conscripts, reservists and volunteers ('Frenchmen of North African stock', in the official jargon). With some honourable exceptions, this political initiative did not work well militarily. The Muslim leadership class, easily targeted for FLN reprisals, generally resisted French efforts to recruit them into the officer corps; and unit cohesion and morale were weakened by the inevitable tensions.

Representative Action, Sector Troops

Before 1959 local military responses to ALN activity were often poorly co-ordinated between sub-sectors, allowing the enemy to take refuge with relative ease in an 'adjoining map square'. Apart from routine security operations, the hunt for the ALN in its sector was often left largely to a unit's attached *harkis* – locally recruited auxiliaries, of whom some

30,000 were already serving by 1959 – under the direction of a few veteran professionals. From 1959, if the 'Challe Steamroller' visited their sectors, garrison units would find themselves galvanised into an unaccustomed tempo of field operations; and those units deployed near the frontiers always ran more chance of combat than those in the centre of the country. As an example of the former we may cite the 1ère Section, 7e Compagnie, 2e Battaillon, 152e Régiment d'Infanterie from the Colmar region of eastern France.

In 1957 the 2e Bn. of the *'quinze-deux'* provided the dispersed garrisons for the Sedrata *sous-secteur*, ZEC. The battalion's 7e Cie was responsible for the Lavest Farm *sous-quartier* of the sub-sector: three villages and about 8,000 inhabitants of a region of some 170 square kilometres of arid plateau. During 1957 the company's first platoon recorded 20 clashes with the enemy, mostly trivial; 11 guerrillas were killed, two taken prisoner, and 15 suspected local FLN agents arrested; four German sub-machine guns and three rifles were recovered.

Early in January 1958 the warrant officer leading this 1ère Section heard that an ALN party was waiting at Kéberit village to guide a katiba crossing from Tunisia. On 7 January at 1330hrs the platoon – 22 men in one half-track and one GMC truck – approached Kéberit, and saw armed men fleeing to take cover in the dry water-course of the Oued Kéberit. A running firefight followed; two ALN were killed and an MG42 and a rifle recovered. From the cover of the gulch the enemy – the 150-strong unit which had crossed from Tunisia the previous night – brought the patrol under heavy and accurate fire; both vehicles were knocked out. The platoon took cover around them and returned fire. The warrant officer attempted to call up reinforcements; radio communications with 7e Cie proved impossible, but he managed to contact a regional relay station and called for air support.

Within minutes two T-6 Texans arrived, summoned from their routine patrol pattern; spotting multiple targets, they called up reinforcements. By 1500 the platoon leader had managed to radio elements of the 26e RI at Mesloula. At 1600 his own company approached, with a local SAS officer's group, but were pinned down. The 1ère Section now had three wounded and were short of ammunition. A helicopter landed to evacuate the casualties, but the ammunition it brought turned out to be '7.5mm instead of 7.63mm' – the phrase suggesting that the platoon were armed with .30cal US M1 Garands instead of 7.5mm MAS36s (see under Plate C2). The ALN kept up the pressure; one T-6 was hit and driven off, its pilot wounded.

When darkness fell the enemy withdrew. At 2130 two companies of the 26e RI, the 8e Cie and the recce platoon of the II/152e all finally arrived on the scene, and searched the ground with the aid of spotlights from circling aircraft. The ALN left 19 dead on the field, and were later reported to have suffered 25 wounded; the matériel recovered included an MG42, a Vickers MG, a Beretta SMG, four .303in rifles, three wire-cutters insulated to 12,000 volts, half a ton of ammunition and useful documents. (As usual, most enemy casualties' weapons had been taken from the field.) Total French losses were four wounded; and a half-track, a truck, and a T-6 damaged.

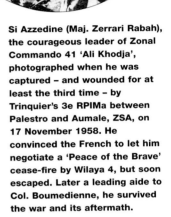

Si Azzedine (Maj. Zerrari Rabah), the courageous leader of Zonal Commando 41 'Ali Khodja', photographed when he was captured – and wounded for at least the third time – by Trinquier's 3e RPIMa between Palestro and Aumale, ZSA, on 17 November 1958. He convinced the French to let him negotiate a 'Peace of the Brave' cease-fire by Wilaya 4, but soon escaped. Later a leading aide to Col. Boumedienne, he survived the war and its aftermath.

'Amirouche the Terrible' (Col. Ait Hamouda), the commander of Wilaya 3 killed on the Djebel Tsameur on 28 March 1959. An effective guerrilla leader, he was also notorious for the hideous cruelty of the purge he unleashed in 1958, partly tricked into it by French intelligence misinformation.

The General Reserve: 'Les Paras'

The mobile reserve of 'intervention' units was based on the 10e and 25e Divisions Parachutistes. These were joined from September 1959 by the 11e Division d'Infanterie (later, Groupement Tactique 11) which was made up of the motorised infantry 3e & 5e REI and 13e DBLE and the armoured 1er REC of the Foreign Legion, and at one time the 29e Tirailleurs. At various dates the reserve could also call upon additional mechanised units, Navy and Air Force Commandos, etc.

The crack airborne regiments received the lion's share of good men, experienced NCOs and officers, modern weapons, transport and radios, up-to-the-minute training, access to operational intelligence, and helicopter lift capacity. They were thus able to perfect aggressive, focused and highly mobile tactics; they played the major role in stopping dead the ALN's attempt to reinforce and resupply the Wilayas from Tunisia and Morocco in winter 1957-spring 1958; and having done so, they provided Gen. Challe with a lethally efficient weapon for hunting down and destroying the dwindling and undersupplied ALN units in the interior during 1959-60.

The para units were divided between Metropolitan regiments (Régiments de Chasseurs Parachutistes, RCP); Colonial regiments (Régiments de Parachutistes Coloniaux, RCP), which were retitled Marine regiments (Régiments Parachutistes d'Infanterie de Marine,

A well set-up company of the ALN's 'Army of the Frontiers', c.1960, parade in French green and camouflage fatigues, caps, and berets; note FM24/29s and MAT49s. French officialdom insisted on calling such fighters merely 'outlaws' (*hors-la-loi*, HLL) throughout the war; French soldiers called them *'fells'* – short for *fellaghas* – and were under no illusions about them.

A French captain with a unit motorised in jeeps and Dodge trucks, photographed during Operation 'Jumelles' in July 1959, when Gen. Challe sent 25,000 troops into Kabylia. He wears a net-covered M1951 helmet, a desert *chêche* scarf and M1947 fatigues, and carries a folding-stock M1A1 US carbine; note metal rank clips on his shoulderstraps and unit *écusson* on his left sleeve.

Col. Houari Boumedienne (left) – former CO of Wilaya 5, and ALN chief-of-staff from Jan. 1960 – in Tunisia, 1962; note also the troops' Egyptian camouflage uniforms and Italian helmets. The SKS rifles supplied to the Tunis-based army were the only Soviet bloc weapons received in any quantity; basically hostile to Communism, the ALN suppressed the local party when it showed signs of taking up arms. The austere, incorruptible Boumedienne finally took power in 1965 to end the internal feuding which tore Algeria apart after independence, ruling with Cromwellian rectitude until his death from cancer in 1978.

RPIMa) in December 1958; and Foreign Legion regiments (Régiments Étrangers de Parachutistes, REP). Essentially these units were identical apart from their berets and insignia, although some details of internal organisation varied.

The reputation won by the paratroopers in Indochina was not tarnished by their defeat against hopeless odds at Dien Bien Phu in spring 1954; but the need to replace them in Indochina in 1954-55, and on-going security operations in Tunisia and Morocco, left few units immediately available for Algeria. The army had been legally unable to send conscripts to SE Asia, and the heavy losses there among professional soldiers – particularly junior leaders – now caused serious problems. It is not generally understood that the majority of the rank and file of the non-Foreign Legion *troupes aeroportées* in Algeria were short-term conscripts, though mixed with some three-year volunteers, recalled reservists, and an often battle-proven professional cadre.

To bring young conscripts – even those who had volunteered for jump training – to the standards of fitness, skill and morale required for airborne intervention units was no easy task; that it was achieved was a tribute to the remarkable leadership of the 'brotherhood' of para colonels who emerged from the tempering fire of Indochina. Famous names included Bigeard and Trinquier (3e RPC), Jeanpierre (1er REP), Ducournau (who led the three-battalion Airborne Group during winter 1954-55), Fossey-François and Chateau-Jobert (2e RPC), Brechignac (9e RCP), and Romain-Desfossés (6e RPC).

The first 18 months saw a complex pattern of tours in Algeria by airborne elements of varying strength and composition drawn from the 25e DIAP (25th Airborne Infantry Division) and the Colonial troops. For instance, the 8e BPC was of mixed regulars, conscripts and recalled reservists; the 1er BPC had entirely career soldiers; and the 2e BPC (from August 1955 redesignated 6e RPC) incorporated many African volunteers from the 6e Tirailleurs Sénégalais. It was only after the distraction of the Suez affair in November 1956 that the classic pattern of the airborne 'fire brigades' truly emerged.

Unit and Divisional Organisation

A reorganisation of French tactical units began in the mid-1950s. Formerly the infantry regiment consisted of two or three battalions usually serving separately (apart from the 1er RCP, all para units were single autonomous battalions). Each normally had three rifle companies and a combined headquarters, services and heavy weapons company, often with a local auxiliary company. During 1955-56 most intervention battalions were redesignated regiments, the term now signifying strong single-battalion combat groups each of an HQ and services company,

A 2e REP casualty is evacuated in a Sikorsky S-55 (H-19). By 1958 some 40 of the similar but larger S-58 (H-34), with space for 12 infantry, were already available for tactical transport and escort – gunship versions were fitted with dual 12.7mm MGs and a 20mm cannon.

four rifle companies, a heavy weapons company and a reconnaissance squadron; motorised regiments often had two tactical HQs so that they could operate in two separate combat groups.

The basic structure of the 1,200-man parachute infantry regiment from 1955 was as follows:

Headquarters
Command & Services Company (CCS)
Six officers, four NCOs, 157 men, 40 vehicles in command, HQ, administrative, signals, transport and medical platoons.

Support Company (CA)
Six officers, 19 NCOs, 117 men, 25 vehicles in command, mortar (3 x 120mm, 6 x 81mm) and anti-tank (4 x jeep-mounted 75mm RCL) platoons.

Reconnaissance Squadron
Five officers, 17 NCOs, 88 men, 33 vehicles in command (12 jeeps) and three recce platoons (each with seven jeeps).

Four Rifle Companies
Each with six officers, 23 NCOs, 184 men and three vehicles in one command and support (1 x 57mm RCL) and four rifle platoons (each with two LMGs).

Most of the active regiments were divided between the two Parachute Divisions. While their role was by definition 'nomadic', and their mission might take them anywhere in the country, the 10e DP initially operated mostly in the west of Algeria and the 25e DP in the east. Their basic composition was as follows:

BELOW **It was common for Muslim detainees to be made to carry radios for French foot patrols. Photographed during a rest on the march, this man has been given basic French fatigues. (Courtesy Jim Worden)**

ALGERIAN TROOPS
1: Commando, Commando de Chasse Kimono 36; Ténés, 1959
2: Moghazni, Sections Administrative Specialisées; Grande Kabylie, 1958-59
3: Sergent-chef, 29e Régiment de Tirailleurs; Oranais, 1959

LES PARAS
1: Chasseur, 1er Régiment de Chasseurs Parachutistes; Algiers, February 1957
2: Lieutenant-colonel Marcel Bigeard, 3e Régiment de Parachutistes Coloniaux; Timimoun, November 1957
3: Commando Parachutiste de l'Air, 1957-59

PARA AND CONSCRIPTS
1: RCL gunner, parachute infantry; winter field dress, 1957-60
2: Soldat, 5e Régiment d'Infanterie; winter field dress, 1959
3: Soldat, 81e Bataillon d'Infanterie; summer field dress, 1958

C

1: Soldat de 1ere classe, 152e Régiment d'Infanterie; winter walking-out dress, Constantine, 1957
2: Soldat, 61e Compagnie de Transmissions, HQ 11e Division d'Infanterie; Constantine, autumn 1960
3: Fusilier Marin, 3e Bataillon, 1er Demi-Brigade de Fusiliers Marins; Moroccan frontier, winter 1958
4: Sous-lieutenant, 1er Compagnie, 2e Régiment de Zouaves; Perregaux, 1957

1: Général de Brigade Jacques Massu, 10e Division Parachutiste; Algiers, spring 1957
2: Lieutenant de vaisseau, Commando de Montfort; Oran, 14 July 1959
3: Sous-lieutenant, Commando Georges (Cdo 135); Saida, 1960
4: Soldat, 8e Régiment Parachutiste d'Infanterie de Marine; Tebessa, 1959

ALN
1: Moudjahid, Aurès mountains, February 1955
2: Dhabet el-aouel, Wilaya 1, spring 1958
3: Djoundi, Battle of the Frontiers, winter 1957-58

F

ALN
1: Djoundi, Battle of the Frontiers, spring 1958
2: Zonal commando, 1957-58
3: Machine gunner, winter field dress, 1957-59

SECTIONS ADMINISTRATIVES SPECIALISÉES, 1955-62
1: Lieutenant, SAS
2: Berber caid, Aurès mountains
3: SAS nursing sister, 1958

10e Division Parachutiste

1er RCP (from 1960, 9e RCP)

1er REP

2e RPC/2e RPIMa

3e RPC/3e RPIMa

6e RPC/6e RPIMa

13e RDP (Régiment de Dragons Parachutistes – recce unit, Ferret scout cars)

20e GAP (Groupe d'Artillerie Parachutiste)

Plus: 60e CGAP (airborne engineer company); 60e CQG (staff company); 60e CPT (parachute signals company); GT 507 (transport group); 60e CRD (divisional maintenance company); 60e SRI (supply section); 405e CMP (parachute medical company); PMAH 10e DP (mixed light aircraft/helicopter platoon)

25e Division Parachutiste

9e RCP (from 1960, 1er RCP)

14e RCP

18e RCP

2e REP

8e RPC/ 8e RPIMa

1er RHP (Régiment de Hussards Parachutistes – recce unit)

1/35e RALP (Régt.d'Artillerie Légère Parachutiste)

Plus: 75e CGAP; 75e CQG; 75e CPT; GT 513; 75e CRD; 75e SRI; 75e CMA (airborne medical company); PMAH 25e DP.

These two divisions were disbanded in April 1961 after the 'Generals' Putsch', as were the 1er REP, 14e and 18e RCP.

French motorised and mechanised units – here the 2e RZ, 1957 – used many types of US vehicles supplied since 1943. This M3 half-track served in large numbers, as did the M8 armoured car, Dodge Weapons Carrier and 6x6 patrol vehicles, and GMC 2½ ton trucks. (Courtesy Jean-Luc Delauve)

For much of the war the paratroopers were almost continually committed, as élite light infantry, to exhausting search-and-destroy operations in punishing alpine terrain, in blazing summer and freezing winter alike (Kabylia has 6,000-foot peaks, and snow lies until early summer). They spent many months at a stretch away from their bases operating from tented forward HQs. Trucked into the sector, they would take off across country for long operations, on foot and heavily loaded, sleeping in pup-tents and living on rudimentary combat rations.

Although they typically inflicted on the ALN ten times their own level of casualties, their losses in ugly encounter battles in the thick scrub, rocky gorges, and (particularly hated) deep caves of the highlands were not negligible. The 2e REP, for example, suffered a total of 741 casualties, against 3,650 enemy killed and 538 captured.

Note this typical imbalance of dead to prisoners: it was rare for either side to give quarter in this war. There is no point in denying that before the Peace of the Brave programme to 'turn' disillusioned guerrillas, those encountered under arms were rarely taken alive except for interrogation, and seldom survived long; even thereafter the proportion of captured to killed was low by conventional standards. (It should be remembered that the fate of the few French prisoners taken by the ALN was usually even grimmer, although some were exchanged.)

Sud Alouette IIs and a Vertol H-21 'banana' heavy troop carrier during a para operation in the ZEC. The first dozen H-21s, with a 20-man capacity, arrived in late 1957. During 1958 the *'ventilos'* were often task-grouped in Helicopter Intervention Detachments comprising four H-21s or six H-34s, a command Alouette, and an H-34 'Pirate' gunship. (Courtesy Jim Worden)

Although a number of parachute drops were made in one- or two-company strength, when the paras flew into battle it was normally as helicopter-borne air cavalry – a concept which the French pioneered in this war. In 1954 the French Army had just one helicopter in Algeria; by the end of 1957 a crash acquisition programme had assembled about 80. From 1958 lift capacity and assault tactics were steadily improved; and by the end of the war some 120 transport helicopters were lifting an average of 21,000 troops monthly.

Paras were typically airlifted into combat in one- or two-company strength once the enemy had been located and fixed by troops on the ground; and the helicopters were often held nearby to shift sub-units around the battlefield as the tactical situation developed. By the major operations of 1959-60, French commanders had become expert in the co-ordination and flexible deployment of their resources: 'hunting commandos' to track and locate the ALN unit; radio OPs airlifted onto commanding peaks, working in conjunction with spotter aircraft; mechanised and infantry elements forming the walls of the 'bottle', and helicopter insertion of its paratrooper 'cork'; close liaison with plentiful tactical air support, and with artillery from over the horizon.

Thus the ALN were consistently outfought; and it was these troops, and these tactics, which destroyed their hopes of moving from the guerrilla to the mobile phase of the classic Maoist revolutionary war programme.

Representative Action, Airborne Troops

An early benchmark for the tactical use of helicopter lifts was the fight between ALN Cdo.41 ('Ali Khodja') and the 3e RPC on 23-25 May 1957 near Agounenda, in the foothills fringing the great agricultural plain of the Mitidja south of the capital. In early May Cdo.41 had routed a Spahi unit, killing 60 for the loss of only seven; a fortnight later they ambushed the 5e BTA, killing a captain and 15 men and persuading others to defect. Intelligence suggested that Cdo.41 would now head west, escorting Wilaya 4 commanders to a rendezvous with other forces near Médéa; and Lt. Col. Bigeard picked Agounenda on the Oued Boulbane, a known ALN route, for an ambush. Trucked from their base at Sidi-Ferruch to Hill 895 by 0130hrs on 23 May, Bigeard's 700 paras made a cold, four-hour night approach march over rough terrain under strict noise and light discipline. Before dawn they were in place and concealed. The HQ and mortars were on Hill 1298; the 1st, 2nd and 3rd Cos. and the Recce Sqn. (on foot) were spread over 10km on four crests overlooking the enemy's probable route; the 4th and Support Cos. were in reserve, and helicopters and ground-attack aircraft were on stand-by at Médéa.

At 1030hrs the most northerly and exposed company (3rd, 'Blue', under Capt. Llamby) radioed sighting a large ALN force approaching his position above the north bank of the Oued Boulbane from the east; at 1045 he opened fire. Already warned by a shepherd, Si Azzedine – leading a column of at least three companies – was attempting to outflank the paras from the north. Llamby, his 100 men outnumbered three to one, came under fierce pressure. The helicopters were already on their way; Bigeard immediately ordered the Support Co. lifted onto high ground north of 3rd Company. The first sticks jumped from the doors at 1055; the whole company were in action by 1130. While the 1st and 2nd Cos. force-marched across country to the support of the 3rd, the Sikorskys lifted the unengaged Recce Sqn. and 4th Co. slightly north-east of Llamby's battle.

Unaccountably, the ALN took to the low-lying Oued Boulbane, dominated from higher ground by the paras – 3rd, 4th, Support and Recce – north of it, and 1st, 2nd and HQ to the south. In a series of running battles over some 30 square kilometres, which lasted 48 hours, Cdo.41 and at least two other katibas made several vigorous counterattacks which came to hand-to-hand fighting. Despite the support of tactical aircraft the paras were too thinly stretched to maintain a tight cordon, however, and some 200 ALN eventually managed to slip away. They left 96 dead and a dozen prisoners, but carried off all but 45 weapons and most of their wounded; the paras lost eight dead and 29 wounded.

If the French were encouraged by the success of battlefield air portability, the ALN took from Agounenda the lesson that large-scale confrontations in the heart of the country must in future be avoided at all costs. Even when they did occur, however, the paras did not always pay such a low price for victory. For instance, during the 'Battle of Souk-Ahras' just inside the Morice Line on 29 April 1958, the 3e Cie./9e RCP, air-lifted onto the Djebel Mouadjene, was surrounded by superior numbers in thick brush which hampered air support, and suffered nearly 30% dead and 30% wounded.

Para-hussars of the 1/1er RHP parade in the field, with squadron *fanion* mounted in a rifle muzzle. Recce elements often fought on foot, leaving their armoured cars at base. These men wear Bigeard caps; M1947/56 camouflage fatigues, the trousers with brown secondary pattern overprinting the green primary; blue squadron scarf at left shoulder; M1950 TAP webbing with, foreground, hand grenade and MAT49 pouches; all have field dressings taped to the left suspender.

ABOVE **Two central elements of the Challe Plan: OPs inserted on commanding crests, and close air support. Fitted with machine guns and rockets, 300 of these T-6 Texan trainers dispersed in independent flights were the backbone of the very effective *Armée de l'Air* tactical effort; P-47 Thunderbolts, B-26 Invaders, and later A-1 Skyraiders and T-28 Trojans were also employed. (Courtesy Jim Worden)**

Paras with a man-portable 57mm 'recoilless rifle' *canon sans recul,* (CSR) near the 'Morice Line'. US M1 and French M1951 helmets were often worn by airborne units during the frontier battles. (Courtesy Jim Worden)

Mutiny, April 1961

The mutiny of April 1961 cannot be passed over without comment. Many field-grade and warrant officers of the intervention units were fighting their third war in 20 years of virtually non-stop active service in Europe, South-East Asia and North Africa. All had learned to despise politicians; and by 1961 the select few who had reached the forefront of their profession were probably the most battle-hardened combat leaders in the world. They had worked tirelessly to create their magnificent battalions; they had driven the enemy from the field; they had been promised that France would never abandon Algeria's Europeans and loyal Muslims.

When the authority of Paris collapsed in May 1958, huge European demonstrations in Algiers had called for the army to take power, and some officers had joined *colon* leaders on Committees of Public Safety. When De Gaulle returned to power he transferred many such 'politicised' officers. He understood that short-term military victory, achieved by ruthless methods which alienated all moderate opinion, had no future. He hoped that patient concessions would buy some future for the *colons* in a semi-independent Algeria, which he would negotiate with the FLN from a position of unassailable military dominance, while remaining evasive about his intentions.

When the para 'centurions' finally understood that – despite everything they had suffered and achieved – outright victory was to be denied them by the man they believed they had brought to power, their sense of betrayal was bitter. Isolated from the increasingly sickened mood of the French public at large (whose sons provided the conscript sector troops), some para officers had come to regard this as their own private war. The mutiny of April 1961 was not thought through in any detail: it was a spasm of rage, which had no achievable long-term objective.

Jubilant paras examine captured weapons after a winter clash in the eastern hills, 1958; note quilted jackets and woollen toques. Visible among the weapons are MG34s, FM24/29s, Beretta MP1938s and an MP40. Apart from French types, German WWII small arms acquired from Czechoslovakia and Yugoslavia dominated the ALN arsenal.

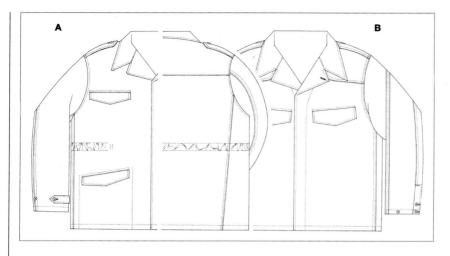

This tragedy, and the purges which followed, poisoned French army morale for decades; and – most significantly – destroyed France's negotiating position with the FLN, hastening the very end which the mutineers had sought to prevent. Many of those involved were men of unquestionable honour; it was a further tragedy that some (though far from all) later became associated with the murderous gangsterism of the OAS.

Postscript

At the time of writing (February 1997) an insurrection by the fundamentalist Islamic Armed Group (GIA) against the government of the Algerian Republic has been raging since 1992; deaths so far total something between 80,000 and 100,000 men, women and children. There is documented evidence for the revival of all the worst horrors of 1954-62: in the towns, assassinations and random bombings; in the countryside, atrocious massacres and mutilations; by the security forces, torture, summary killings and reprisals. The reader may recall the author's comment at the beginning of this text, that the events of 1954-62 were shaped more by local factors than by any general theory of revolutionary or counter-insurgency warfare.

Schematic drawings of French M1947 fatigues: (A) four-pocket jacket, (B) two-pocket 'lightened' shirt/jacket, (C) trousers. These were all produced in both drab green and, under the 'all arms' designation, camouflage pattern. (Christa Hook)

SELECT BIBLIOGRAPHY

Bail, René, *Hélicoptères et Commandos-Marine en Algérie*, Charles-Lavauzelle (1983)

Gaujac, Paul, (ed.), *Histoire des Parachutistes Français*, Éditions de l'Albatros/SPL (1975)

Horne, Alistair, *A Savage War of Peace: Algeria 1954-62*, Macmillan (1977)

Huré, Gen. R. (ed.), *L'Armée d'Afrique 1830-1962*, Charles-Lavauzelle (1977)

Leulliette, Pierre, *St Michael and the Dragon*, Heinemann (1964)

Massu, Jacques, *La Vraie Bataille d'Alger*, Plon (1971)

Murray, Simon, *Legionnaire*, Sidgwick & Jackson (1978)

Simon, J., *L'Infanterie d'Afrique 1830-1962*, L'Association Symboles & Tradition (1979)

Worden, James, *The Wayward Legionnaire*, Robert Hale (1988)

For the colour plate references I have drawn heavily upon the published researches of D.Lassus, J.Sicard and P.Pivetta in various issues of *Militaria* Magazine (particularly Nos. 3, 4, 7, 8, 9, 10, 99, 102, 106, 126, 132 & 133), and wish to acknowledge my great debt to them. Published by Histoire & Collections, 5 Avenue de la République, 75011 Paris, France, under the editorship of M.Philippe Charbonnier and the overall direction of my greatly respected colleague M.Francois Vauvillier, *Militaria* is in my opinion simply the best uniform history journal in the world.

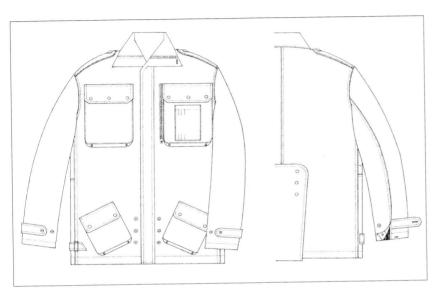

Schematic drawings of French airborne troops' camouflage smock M1947/53. (Christa Hook)

BELOW **Schematic drawings of French airborne troops' camouflage smock M1947/56. (Christa Hook)**

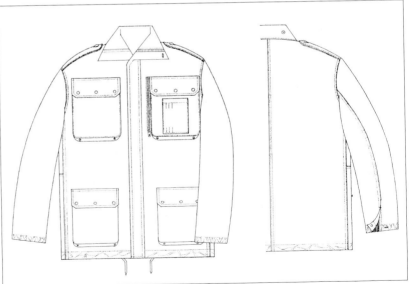

THE PLATES

Note: Although the Foreign Legion played a prominent part in French operations, no Legion figures are included here; see extensive material in Elite 6 *French Foreign Legion Paratroops* and Men-at-Arms 300 *French Foreign Legion since 1945*.

The most common uniforms were the French M1947 *treillis de combat* or *tenue de campagne* (combat fatigues) in drab green and later in camouflage finish: and the series of camouflage fatigues for airborne troops. The green fatigues, the almost universal working dress of French forces throughout the war, were also acquired in quantity by the ALN. The 'all-arms' camouflage version became increasingly common from the late 1950s, replacing the green set in many French units.

The similarly camouflaged airborne troops' fatigues were worn throughout the war. There was some variation in the exact printing of the basically similar streaked camouflage patterns of various shades of green and brown on light green (or less often, khaki drab) backgrounds; this was due to dispersed mass production, and was not significant – smocks and trousers of differing appearance were often worn together.

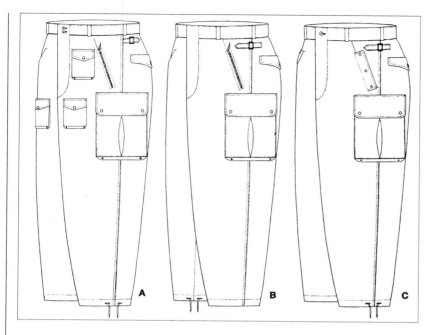

Schematic drawings of French airborne troops' camouflage trousers: (A) M1947/52, (B) M1947/53, (C) M1947/56. (Christa Hook)

The airborne *tenue de saut camouflée* went through several slightly varying versions, worn indiscriminately in Algeria. The main identifying features of the various smocks were as follows *Veste M1947/51* – Deep Denison-type collar; external breast pockets, three-snap flaps, drainage eyelets, left pocket with zipped internal access via inner vertical edge and pencil pocket on face; smaller skirt pockets slanting inwards at bottom, two-snap flaps, drainage eyelets; vertical zipped vents either side of upper back; two inwards-slanting internal rear skirt pockets, pointed single-snap flaps; forward-buttoning hip and wrist tabs; Denison-type 'beaver tail' secured to three pairs of snaps front or back. *Veste M1947/52* – Collar smaller; no rear pockets or zipped vents; broader wrist tabs with sliding-clamp buckles. *Veste M1947/53* – Collar smaller; forward-buttoning wrist tabs; smaller hip tabs with sliding-clamp buckles. *Veste M1947/54* – 'Beaver tail' removed (and often cut off earlier smocks by individuals).*Veste M1947/56* – Skirt pockets enlarged, set vertically, three-snap flaps; wrist and hip tabs removed; drawstring hem; wrists elasticated; buttons under collar for optional hood.

The trousers – worn indiscriminately with matching or any other models of smock – differed progressively as follows: *Pantalon M1947/51* – Buckled tab at front waistband; two slash side pockets, the left zip-fastened; two internal rear pockets, pointed single-snap flaps; two bellows cargo pockets on outside thighs, drainage eyelets, two-snap flaps; three small pockets on front thighs (two left, one right), drainage eyelets, pointed single-button flaps. *Pantalon M1947/52* – Two buttons at front waistband; hip tabs adjusting backwards with sliding-clamp buckles. *Pantalon M1947/53 and /54* – Small thigh pockets removed; forward-buckling hip tabs; minor waistband differences. *Pantalon M1947/56* – Side pockets covered by slanting three-snap flaps, left pocket zip removed.

The green M1947 jacket had a fold-down collar, and four internally hung pockets with pointed external flaps; the trousers had slash side and flapped rear pockets, and large cargo pockets on the outside thighs; apart from those for the shoulder straps and wrist and ankle tightening tabs, all buttons were concealed. An M1947/52 variation had externally mounted skirt pockets. In 1952 a 'lightened' – *allegée* – shirt/jacket version also appeared, with breast pockets only, buttoned cuffs, and (often) a doubled shoulder yoke; this was worn either inside or outside the trousers.

The 'all-arms' camouflage version, *tenue de combat camouflée modèle 1947 toutes armes*, was authorised in 1954 but not widely available for some time. Originally identical to the green set, it acquired external jacket skirt pockets almost at once. A two-pocket 'lightened' version with reinforced shoulder yoke was also produced.

Two sets of personal equipment were widely used in Algeria. The M1946 brown leather set with black metal fittings consisted of a waistbelt, Y-straps, a rear connector, and various alternative holsters and pouches; the most common were doubled rifle ammunition pouches, and pairs of magazine pouches for the MAT49 sub-machine gun. This set was most commonly used by the 'sector' troops.

Schematic of typical camouflage pattern on khaki or - more often - light green ground. The primary colour (dark tone) was more often green, the secondary (mid-tone) brown, and the primary printed over the secondary, but reversals of all these were known.

The web equipment *type TAP* ('*troupes aeroportées*') was usually (though not universally, nor exclusively) issued to the paras and other intervention units. This comprised a waistbelt with eyelets and various types of quick-release buckle, adjustable suspenders crossing at the rear, a web carrier for a US-type canteen, a large first-aid pouch, doubled rifle ammo pouches, pairs of five-pocket MAT49 magazine pouches, a similar slightly smaller pouch for rifle grenades, a US-style three-pocket grenade pouch with leg ties, etc. Both equipment sets were seen in use by the ALN. World War II vintage US Army webbing items were also still in quite widespread use by both sides.

A: ALGERIAN TROOPS

Most Muslim troops were divided between the traditional regular units of the Army of Africa – the *tirailleurs* and *spahis algériens*; the *harkis* – auxiliaries locally raised as extra platoons and companies by many French units; from 1959, the *commandos de chasse* (tracking units), often partly composed of 'turned' ALN fighters; and the *moghazni* auxiliaries raised and led by district officers of the SAS (see under Plate H1).

A1: Commando, Commando de Chasse Kimono 36; Ténès, 1959 In December 1958 Gen. Challe ordered the raising of 'hunting commandos'; by April 1959 there were about 25 in each army corps, and in time at least 150 would be affiliated to French sector units. Most had about 140 men, but some *commandos légers* had only about 70. Between 30% and 60% of the rank and file were Muslim volunteers, including veterans of regular units, *harkis*, and 'turned' ALN fighters – of which there was no shortage. There was a higher than usual proportion of French cadre, drawn either from the 'parent' unit or from several in that sector.

The commandos' task was to cut the tracks of locally active ALN units, and to follow them for however long it took and wherever they led. Keeping in frequent contact with base, they were to 'mark their men' (Gen. Challe was a rugby enthusiast) while the intervention units got into place to

An American corporal of the 3e REI who served in Algeria under the name Donald Thomas. He wears the green beret adopted by Legion infantry c.1960; and the two-pocket shirt/jacket variant of the 'all-arms' camouflage fatigues, with a rank tab (two green stripes on dark blue) hanging from a button. (Courtesy Jim Worden)

surround, fix, and wipe out the *katiba*. With good fieldcraft skills and local knowledge, these commandos were often highly effective. Algiers Army Corps commandos were coded either 'K-Kimono' or 'P-Partisan' followed by a number; K36 was affiliated to the III/22e RI at Ténès, ZOA.

Green or camouflage fatigues were issued, with Bigeard caps or camouflage berets, but not bush hats or helmets. Equipment, and weapons including LMGs but nothing heavier, were standard issue; but note dagger made from cut-down German Mauser bayonet. The North African hooded woollen robe – *djellaba* – was carried as a greatcoat/blanket. Commandos, *harkis*, and French recce parties quite often disguised themselves in full or outer native clothing.

A2: Moghazni, Sections Administratives Specialisées; Grande Kabylie, 1958-59 Mounted cavalry were quite widely used in Algeria; in very broken terrain a horse is more capable than a vehicle, quieter, easier to refuel, and gives a better view. The district officers of the SAS were given the means to recruit and train a *maghzen*, 30 to 40 strong. Fatigue uniforms and equipment were issued, in this case the M1948 khaki shirt, green M1947 trousers, M1917 boots, and M1935 belt equipment.

The usual distinguishing headgear (as among the *harkis*) was the all-red M1946 *bonnet de police*, and the subject photograph also shows plain red shoulderboards. The French army's standard issue 7.5mm MAS36 bolt-action rifle was a rather flimsily built weapon; it took only five rounds, and had no safety catch. Horses and saddlery were locally obtained.

A3: Sergent-chef, 29e Régiment de Tirailleurs; Oranais, 1959 This career NCO leading an urban patrol, no doubt a veteran of World War II and Indochina, wears the M1957 *bonnet de police* ('calot') in RTA branch colours of pale blue and yellow, with the two diagonals of his rank as a brass pin-on badge. A full double chevron in brass is – unusually – pinned to the left breast of his 'lightened' M1947 fatigue shirt/jacket; and the 29e RTA badge is fobbed to the right pocket button. Two double magazine pouches for the widely-used US M1 carbine are carried on his French M1946 leather belt, and another on the butt of his weapon; he also carries

Moroccan *tirailleur* of the 9e RTM in field uniform, 1956: green M1947 fatigues over olive crew-neck sweater, M1945 web anklets, M1950 belt, with a white *chèche* wrapped tightly into a turban – 'Indian-style'. (Courtesy Jean-Luc Delauve)

41

A young French *aspirant* (officer candidate – two black bars across single rank lace on shoulders, *sous-lieutenant* rank lace on cap) wearing Zouave sidecap and M1946 battle-dress. The *écusson* of the 2e RZ on his sleeve is gold on midnight blue with the triple edging (here in red) of units of the traditional Army of Africa; the regiment's citation lanyard is in yellow flecked with green, the ribbon colours of the Médaille Militaire. See under Plates D1 & D4. (Courtesy Jean-Luc Delauve)

OF37 hand grenades. M1945 web anklets are worn with rubber-soled M1945 brown leather boots.

B: LES PARAS

B1: Chasseur, 1er Régiment de Chasseurs Parachutistes, 10e Division Parachutiste; Maison-Carrée, Algiers, February 1957 During the 'Battle of Algiers' Lt. Col. Meyer's 1er RCP took control of the eastern sector of the city. For urban duty this paratrooper wears only an unsupported belt with one set of MAT49 pouches balanced by a canteen behind his other hip. The rifle section was divided into a fire team, with the 7.5mm LMG (initially the old magazine-loaded FM24/29, later the belt-fed AA52) and ammo carriers armed with rifles, and an assault team of *voltigeurs* armed with this excellent 9mm SMG. His camouflage fatigues are of M1947/52 and /53 patterns; the boots are M1952 'rangers', at this date issued in brown and overpolished black to give this dark shade. From 1954 the Metropolitan *chasseurs parachutistes* reverted from red to the royal blue beret which marked their pre-World War II Air Force origins; this was worn until September 1957 (see under Plate E4). The Air Force

colours of royal blue and orange-yellow are also seen in the *écusson*, the diamond-shaped insignia of branch and unit worn on the left sleeve of service dress and sometimes displayed on fatigues. Parachute wings (for eight jumps) and regimental badge are pinned to the right breast and pocket. Insignia would not generally be worn in the field, though some photos show paras on operations displaying divisional shoulder patches.

B2: Lieutenant-colonel Marcel Bigeard, 3e Régiment de Parachutistes Coloniaux; Timimoun, November 1957 Bigeard – 'Bruno', from his long-time radio callsign – was a famous member of the élite circle of paratroop colonels. A charismatic leader, highly decorated for Maquis service in World War II and for his command of the 6e BPC in Indochina, he had been prominent in the defence of Dien Bien Phu. He returned from a Viet Minh prison camp in September 1954; and under his command the 3e RPC achieved many successes, both in the *bled* and the Algiers casbah. This is the pose in which he was often photographed: crouched over a map, surrounded by SCR300 radios, orchestrating his companies' movements on foot, by truck and by helicopter. Bigeard commanded the Subversive and Guerrilla Warfare Instruction Centre in 1958, and the Saida sector of the Sud-Oranais from 1959.

In Indochina late in 1953 he devised the field cap which army slang would name after him, copying the Word War II Japanese and Afrika Korps equivalents; by 1957 it had become regulation issue to the RCPs and RPCs, and was worn by various other intervention units (captured caps were much prized by the ALN). It is made from standard French camouflage cloth; but Bigeard's personal uniform for this Saharan operation was a heavily modified suit of British M1942 windproof camouflage – 'sausage skin', a material popular in Indochina for its coolness. (Photos of his men during this operation show standard camouflage smocks and caps worn with khaki shorts.) His only insignia is a chest rank patch, his only equipment a US M1936 pistol belt and a pair of old Afrika Korps tinted plastic goggles.

B3: Commando Parachutiste de l'Air, 1957-59 The General Reserve's need for high-quality recce and intervention units led to a call for Air Force volunteers in March 1956. By May 'Commando 10', the 150 survivors of punishing selection training, were ready for combat orientation;

Cdos.20 and 30 were operational by October, and Cdos.40 and 50 in February 1957 and February 1959 respectively. In April 1957 the first three, grouped as the GCPA at Reghaia and Boufarik air bases, became a helicopter intervention unit for the Corps d'Armée d'Alger.

They specialised in long fighting patrols, typically being inserted by helicopter on a suspected ALN route and remaining concealed in ambush for days if necessary; when contact was made they were highly skilled at co-operation with tactical aircraft. (The Air Commandos also provided door gunners for S-58/H-34 gunship helicopters, manning 12.7mm/.50cal machine guns, and German MG151 20mm aircraft cannon rigged on pedestal mounts.)

In the field Air Commandos wore para fatigues with a camouflage cap of flatter outline than the Bigeard type; when not tactical they wore the *bleu roi* Air Force beret with a gold badge. His M1950 TAP web equipment includes two pairs of *cartouchières* M1950/53, and the large 'commando type' first-aid pouch. The 7.5mm MAS49/56 self-loading rifle, with integral grenade launcher and detachable ten-round magazine, replaced the MAS36 in intervention units from about 1957. Taped to his heavily loaded M1951 all-arms *bergram* rucksack is an air visibility panel; these were also seen in yellow/black bars and white/red triangles, the colours being reversed on the other side, and sometimes bore additional recognition letters.

C1: RCL gunner, parachute infantry; winter field dress, 1957-60

This para from the command and support platoon of a rifle company manhandles the American 57mm 'recoilless rifle'; despite its 22kg (48.5lb) weight and the disadvantage of its highly visible back-blast, its 3kg (6.6lb) fragmentation round was valuable for delivering fire into caves, gullies and other heavy cover. He wears the Bigeard cap with the split neck flap down (it was usually tucked up inside), M1947/52 and /53 jump fatigues, M1950 webbing and jump boots. In cold weather a quilted, collarless, long-sleeved olive drab jacket was often worn under the smock. His personal weapon is the 9mm MAC50 pistol in one of two versions of the M1950 web holster; his canteen is the M1952. An air visibility panel is taped to his web knapsack *(musette d'allégement* M1950/51). Note also the coloured scarf tied at the shoulder as a field identification sign; usually in red, blue, green, yellow or white, these were widely worn throughout the French forces at the shoulder or neck (or both, in contrasting colours), the position and colour changing according to operation orders. At Agounenda the heavily engaged 3e Cie., 3e RPC were 'blue company'.

The silver Airborne Forces beret badge - see under Plates B1 and E1.

M1946 battledress with the Foreign Legion's special creases, worn for a decoration parade by the CO of the 2e REP and one of his sergeant-majors (three gold chevrons above Legion *écusson* with gold seven-flame grenade, triple green edging). Note five alternating gold/silver *galons* of the lieutenant-colonel's rank around the top edge of his black *képi*. (Courtesy Jim Worden)

C2: Soldat, 5e Régiment d'Infanterie; winter field dress, 1959

This conscript serving with the sector troops wears the French M1951 steel helmet; it was also common to wear the fibre liner alone. The M1947/52 fatigues have external skirt pockets; it was unusual but not unknown for the midnight blue M1945 *écusson* to be worn in the field. This bears the nine-flame grenade of the infantry below the unit number, within the double edging of Metropolitan (and Colonial) units, all in red. The trousers are gathered into the US-inspired M1951 web gaiters, over M1945 boots. His M1946 leather equipment includes belt, braces, and two double rifle ammunition pouches. The 5e RI were one of many sector units which carried US small arms; photos show the M1 Garand, M3 'grease gun' and BAR in widespread use as well as the ubiquitous M1 carbine, thus complicating ammunition resupply. Jackal and fox cubs were popular pets.

C3: Soldat, 81e Bataillon d'Infanterie; summer field dress, 1958

This sector unit provided a weak company for an isolated post at Guentis in the arid Nemencha Mountains of the south-east Constantinois. Armed with an MAS36, this conscript wears the lightest kit for local duty in summer – perhaps standing guard over the weekly market in the Muslim village. The M1949 fabric bush hat was seen in both the original sand-khaki and later drab green. The M1948 khaki shirt has its sleeves shortened here; it is worn with matching shorts, and canvas and rubber *pataugas*. The M1946 leather belt and pouches are worn without braces, and with the webbing carrier of the M1951 canteen looped on at the back.

Typical of the high quality of French regimental breast badges, that of the 9e RCP is of scarlet enamel with gold details and a dull gold figure of St. Michael, patron saint of paratroopers.

D1: Soldat de 1ère classe, 2e Bataillon, 152e Régiment d'Infanterie; winter walking-out dress, Constantine, 1957
This recalled reservist wears on the left front of his M1957 *calot* – for the infantry, midnight blue with red top fold and piping – the red enamelled diagonal bar of his rank. His M1946 wool serge battledress is worn *en tenue de sortie*, with the added shoulderboards of his branch and the collective citation lanyard of his regiment; daily barracks dress, *tenue No. 3*, dispensed with these, but still displayed the *écusson*; the infantry grenade is repeated on the shoulderboards. His single rank chevron in red on midnight blue butts down against the diamond on the left sleeve, and is worn alone on the right sleeve with a solid triangle of the backing in the bight. The 152e wore the citation *fourragère* of the Légion d'Honneur. Fobbed to the right pocket is the enamelled regimental badge of the 152e, 'Les Diables Rouges'. He wears the khaki shirt with a slightly darker tie; and civilian-style shoes.

The uniforms of Muslims locally recruited into French Metropolitan and Colonial units were distinguished on formal occasions by a broad red waist sash worn under the leather belt.

D2: Soldat, 61e Compagnie de Transmissions, HQ 11e Division d'Infanterie; Constantine, autumn 1960 Divisional patches were not widely worn for other than parade occasions. That of the 11e DI was issued from February 1957: a white-bladed sword with yellow and black hilt on a red shield set on a pale blue backing bordered with black. It is worn here on M1947 all-arms camouflage fatigues by a soldier of the divisional signals company; an enamelled company badge is pinned to the right pocket. A black beret is worn with a yellow metal version of the sword insignia – a non-regulation affectation. (Perhaps, in a division now almost entirely composed of Foreign Legion units, the signallers felt the need to cut a bit of a dash, too.)

D3: Fusilier Marin, 3e Bataillon, 1er Demi-Brigade de Fusiliers Marins; Moroccan frontier, winter 1958 The 3,000-strong 1er DBFM was formed in July 1956 from conscripts. With HQ at Nemours, ZOO, the three battalions (and their formidable locally recruited 'Commando Yatagan') were responsible for some 800 square kilometres. Although the Tunisian border was the greater threat, the western 'barrage' – stretching from the coast via Marnia, Ain-Sefra and Beni-Ounif south to Colomb-Béchar – got plenty of attention from the ALN in Morocco. From 1959 the DBFM's 1er Bn. joined the General Reserve; the 3e patrolled the barrage itself, and the 2e provided defence in depth further east.

This composite figure, from photos of a half-track crew, wears M1947 fatigues with the DBFM's left sleeve patch and naval headgear; a woollen toque; US M1955 body armour; and a US M1 helmet painted with a red anchor (the photographed crew wear a mixture of these and French M1951 helmets). The chest pouch rig for five SMG magazines, in bright green canvas and light brown hide, is often seen in photos of both the DBFM and the Naval Commando Group (see Plate E2).

D4: Sous-lieutenant, 1er Compagnie, 2e Régiment de Zouaves; Perregaux, 1957 To the Zouaves, as to the Legion, Algeria was home. The 2e RZ served from autumn 1955 in the ZEO, equipped with US half-tracks. In 1956-58 they operated alongside the Legion's 5e REI; once the eastern Oranais was more or less pacified they adopted the routine of most sector troops – patrols, guarding European farms, trying to protect native villages from FLN pressure, night ambushes on suspected enemy routes, convoy escorts, and 'hearts and minds' missions such as public works and medical aid.

This young officer wears the Zouaves' red *bonnet de police* with a midnight blue top fold; his rank is marked by a single small chevron of gold lace at the cap front, and a single gold horizontal bar on a buttoned-on midnight blue chest tab. His 'lightened' M1947 camouflage fatigue shirt/jacket is worn outside the trousers of the British M1942 windproof camouflage suit (a combination widely seen in photos of this unit, together with the M1951 fibre helmet

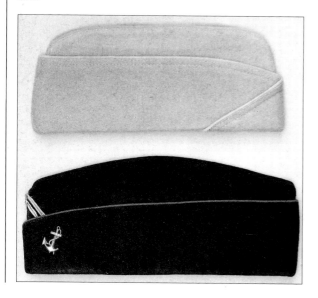

French *bonnets de police*: (top) right side of Tirailleurs Algériens cap, enlisted ranks, M1946, in pale blue with lemon yellow top fold and turn-up piping; (bottom) left side of officer quality Infanterie Coloniale cap, resembling the more rounded shape which would become universal with the M1957, in midnight blue with red piping, lieutenant's two gold lace chevrons, and – broken here – the gold anchor badge of Colonial regiments. (Courtesy Denis Lassus)

liner). He wears a single leather SMG magazine pouch on a US M1936 web pistol belt, and carries an MAT49. Note the unusually robust tropical boots, no doubt a private purchase.

E1: Général de Brigade Jacques Massu, 10e Division Parachutiste; Algiers, spring 1957 A highly decorated veteran of the Liberation and Indochina, Massu stepped onto the world stage in 1957 as general officer commanding the 10e DP when it was called into Algiers city and given a free hand to root out the FLN bombers. His routine sanctioning of torture to extract information remains highly controversial; Massu was always completely straightforward in taking responsibility for what he considered distasteful but unavoidable methods, given his mission and resources. His success made him a hero to the *pieds noirs*; he supported the return of De Gaulle and was completely loyal to him, although his outspoken advocacy of the army's viewpoint got him dismissed as GOC Algiers Army Corps in January 1960. (His promised support for De Gaulle during the Paris riots of May 1968, when commander of French troops in Germany, earned the release of army personnel still in prison for their activities in 1961-62.)

The dark red beret was worn by all French Metropolitan and Colonial para units in Indochina from 1951; from 1954 returning Metropolitan units reverted to royal blue (see Plate B1) while Colonials retained red, all para units still wearing this silver Airborne Forces badge; Massu favoured a large size Colonial beret. His M1947/56 fatigues are modified with a full-length smock zip; his M1950 web belt has the Rapco buckle, and he wore dark brown M1950/53 jump boots. Insignia are his two gold rank stars on black shoulder strap slides, parachutist's wings, the 10e DP patch on the right shoulder, and his impressive array of medal ribbons mounted on black in the French style.

E2: Lieutenant de vaisseau, Commando de Montfort; Oran, 14 July 1959 The Groupement des Commandos-Marine comprised Cdos. de Montfort and Trepel, which arrived from Morocco and Tunisia in 1955, joined in 1956 by Cdos. Jaubert and Penfentenyo; each was the equivalent of a strong company group. Their green beret pulled right in British fashion commemorated the Free French Naval Commandos' exploits in World War II. It was worn, with their distinctive badge, for all duties until *c.*1960, when Bigeard caps were adopted for operations. The GCM characteristically wore camouflage para smocks with green fatigue trousers for all duties until about mid-1959, thereafter wearing full camouflage suits when tactical. A number of photos *c.*1956-59 show smocks in this unusual blotched camouflage instead of the usual streaked pattern, and what appear to be white-lined dark khaki shirts. Rank insignia were naval; for this parade the CO wears naval shoulder boards, the unit's *fourragère* in the yellow and green of the Médaille Militaire ribbon, and full personal decorations; note that the design of the jump smock prevented the lanyards' ferrule ends being carried across to the centre of the breast in the usual parade style.

Soldiers of the 2e Zouaves patrolling near Perregaux in the Oranais, 1957. Both wear M1947 green fatigues, one with the red and blue Zouave sidecap and one with a bush hat. The radios are the US SCR300 and, foreground, SCR536 'handie-talkie'. (Courtesy Jean-Luc Delauve)

The gold beret badge of the Air Force Commandos – see under Plate B3.

E3: Sous-lieutenant, Commando Georges (Cdo 135); Saida, 1960 Some *commandos de chasse* acquired metal breast badges, and a few – e.g. Commando Georges and Commando Cobra, raised largely from former ALN fighters by the I/8e RIMot in the Saida sector, ZSO, in February 1959 – wore shoulder patches at least for parades. (Initially numbered Cdos. 47 and 43, these two units were later redesignated 135 and 134 respectively, indicating affiliation to units of the 13e DI.) A photo of an Algerian officer shows the unit's brass crescent and dagger breast badge; a red and black shoulder patch with gold-lettered 'Georges' (after the founding commander, Lt. Georges Grillet); French rank bars, and a red unit scarf. The 'Medal for Security Operations and Maintenance of Order' was introduced in January 1958 for 90 days' service – it was the Algerian War campaign medal in all but name.

E4: Soldat, 8e Régiment Parachutiste d'Infanterie de Marine; Tebessa, 1959 In September 1957 all Metropolitan para units were ordered back into the red beret; so in June 1958, to distinguish them from the *chasseurs parachutistes*,

LEFT **The dull gold beret badge of the Naval Commando Group – see under Plate E2.**

RIGHT **The beret badge of the Colonial Parachute Regiments from June 1958, a dark silver winged fist and dagger on a gold fouled anchor – see under Plate E4.**

the Colonial units received this new cap badge of the silver winged fist and dagger superimposed on a gold anchor. In December 1958 Colonial units reverted to their historic title of 'Marine regiments'. The use of camouflage fatigues with parade embellishments for formal occasions – such as the parade at which this para has been awarded the Croix de Valeur Militaire, the equivalent of the Croix de Guerre for this 'war that was not a war' – became very marked in the late 1950s. The M1946 shoulderboards in midnight blue bear in red the two small chevrons and fouled anchor of Marine troops, the anchor repeated inside double red edging on the midnight blue sleeve *écusson*. This, like the 25e DP patch on the right shoulder, is temporarily attached with hooks and eyes. The 8e RPC/RPIMa's citation lanyard in the pale blue and red of the ribbon of the Croix de Guerre TOE ('for external theatres of operations') is worn on the left shoulder. Para wings and the 8e RPC/RPIMa unit badge are pinned to the right breast.

F AND G: ARMÉE DE LIBERATION NATIONALE

Although it evolved into a well-supplied guerrilla army, the ALN was never 'uniform' in its clothing and equipment; we illustrate only a sample of the wide variety seen. French fatigues acquired via Tunisia or Morocco gradually became the most common dress, but were never universal; and a huge range of headgear was worn. For instance, a single photo showing about 20 men of one unit in 1958 includes French M1947 and US M1943 fatigues; French bush hats and *bonnets de police*, berets in both green drab and camouflage cloth, and a variety of visored field caps; French, British and US webbing and French leather equipment; Mauser K98 and Garand M1 rifles, and a BAR. We have not illustrated figures of the external forces who only returned to Algeria after the cease-fire. Photos of parades in Tunisia show what appear to be Egyptian airborne camouflage fatigues and Italian M1933 steel helmets, Simonov SKS rifles, and old *Hitlerjugend* daggers as sidearms. (Others show men training with early AK47s and RPGs, but Soviet bloc equipment played virtually no part in the war itself.) Film taken in Tunisia shows some officers wearing complete French camouflage even extending over the visor of a stiff-topped officer's cap, with a brass badge in the shape of a star between the points of an upwards crescent; and applied khaki or camouflage shoulderboards with stars of rank.

F1: Moudjahid, Aurès mountains, February 1955 A fugitive being hunted through the hills by Ducournau's paratroopers during the first winter. A composite of various prisoner photos, he wears the red Berber skullcap and civilian clothes; with this heavy mackinaw-style hunting jacket and corduroys he is probably a good deal better equipped than most. He is armed only with a shotgun, though at close quarters heavy boar-shot could be devastating – and in the mountains many encounters took place at very close quarters.

F2: Dhabet el-aouel, Wilaya 1, spring 1958 A composite, largely from a photo of a fighter captured south of Tebessa by the 2e REP; his weapon is not visible, but given the small size of the rounds in his ammunition belts we have painted him with an M1A1 Thompson, a prestige weapon among the ALN. A *chèche* is rolled into a makeshift turban. The M1939 US Army service tunic appears in many photos; we have added one white and one red star to the shoulder straps for the rank of *dhabet el-aouel*, equivalent to first lieutenant, on the command staff of a katiba. The trousers appear to be French M1948 khaki slacks, and variations on the French issue *pataugas* were widely worn.

F3: Djoundi, Battle of the Frontiers, winter 1957-58 A composite from several photos, illustrating a typical ALN soldier of the middle war years moving up to try to cross the 'barrage'. Various knitted cap-comforters and balaclavas, some with integral visors, were widely used, among them this US Army 'beanie'. The greatcoat is French army issue; and personal equipment options seem to have included six or eight of the pouches, single-size only, from the M1935 set. The most obvious signs of President Nasser's decision to supply the ALN from British surplus stocks in Egypt are the Mk.III steel helmet (smaller numbers of the Mk.II, and the RAC rimless pattern, were also seen); and the SMLE Mk.III rifle. A British No. 36 grenade is carried in the French '*boule* basket' leather carrier.

G1: Djoundi, Battle of the Frontiers, spring 1958 A composite from photos. The ALN wore any French camouflage uniforms they could get, the dress of the famous paras being felt to bestow prestige. This certainly did not come – in the numbers photographed – from French dead, so must have been bought by ALN agents on the open market. This soldier wears the 'lightened, all-arms' version, with a Bigeard cap made from French poncho material. Note pin-on badge, with the ALN's red star-and-crescent on a halved green/white backing, on his left chest; various katiba insignia were also locally produced, but details are unknown, and insignia of any kind were very rare in the field. The US web rifle belt carries ammunition for his Czech-made Mauser K98, by far the most common rifle in ALN service, though the MAS36, Garand, M1 carbine, SMLE and British No. 4 were also used in quantity. Packs were enormously various, and the non-military colour of these straps suggests that this fighter has a locally made rucksack or knapsack.

G2: Zonal commando, 1957-58 This *djoundi* wears a US M1943 field jacket with French M1947 trousers, and one of a number of field cap designs worn indiscriminately within ALN units; others included an Afrika Korps-style high-fronted shape made ugly by the fact that its unstiffened visor flopped sharply down over the eyes, and a 'Mao' or 'railroad engineer' style. His British-style web belt supports an M1951 canteen and leather M1946 SMG magazine pouches. The German MP40 sub-machine gun was widely used, as were the MAT49 and Beretta M1938; rare photos also show a few German Sturmgewehr StG44 assault rifles. The standard ALN left shoulder patch was the most common insignia, though very far from universal.

G3: Machine gunner, winter field dress, 1957-59 This soldier wears a more substantial field cap of woollen cloth, and over his M1947 fatigues, for warmth, the ubiquitous North African *djellaba*. He was photographed crewing a French FM24/29 LMG, but we have substituted the German MG34 which often figured in French after-action photos and reports. The MG42 was less commonly encountered, as was the old Lewis; the FM24/29, Bren, and Browning Automatic Rifle were acquired in quantity; and tripod-mounted machine guns included the Hotchkiss and Vickers. All ALN ammunition resupply was a logistic nightmare.

H: SECTIONS ADMINISTRATIVES SPECIALISÉES, 1955-62

H1: Lieutenant, SAS Created by Governor-General Soustelle in 1955, the SAS was an ambitious 'hearts and minds' initiative to provide villagers with practical help and a visible French presence, improving their lives while pro-

Going home: men of the 2e Zouaves (note badge painted on suitcase) in fully badged battledress *tenue de sortie*. The *caporal-chef* (right – one gold above two red chevrons) has the Zouave crescent and regimental number on his shoulder boards as well as his sleeve *écusson*. (Jean-Luc Delauve)

Probably photographed after the 1962 cease-fire, two ALN men chat to villagers. One wears a beret in French camouflage material and what appear to be Egyptian airborne camouflage fatigues. The outfit on the right resembles French camouflage, but shows vertical rather than horizontal streaks. Khaki, green and various French coloured sidecaps were worn by the ALN, sometimes with added badges.

tecting them from intimidation. Some 400 small volunteer teams were led by Arabic-speaking junior officers with local knowledge. Generously funded, the programme covered public health, education, building, agricultural assistance and administration of justice, as well as local counter-insurgency intelligence and liaison with the armed forces. Many of these '*képis bleus*' were admirably devoted and courageous men; in remote posts, protected only by a handful of local auxiliaries, their real popularity with the Muslim villagers made them prime targets of the FLN. This officer wears the sky-blue cap, dark red shoulderboards and sleeve badge, and gold crescent-and-star insignia of the SAS with the M1948 khaki shirtsleeve uniform; he carries a Kabylie girl child wearing typically colourful local costume.

H2: Berber caid, Aurès mountains The type of Muslim whose plight – caught between the army and the FLN, neither of which could protect the remote villages from the other, but both of which inflicted reprisals for 'collaboration' – was perhaps the most pitiable of all. He wears a typical mixture of local dress and European cast-offs; the colourful straw hat was a regional speciality. His medals mark him as a Tirailleur veteran of one or both World Wars. Basic weapons, including ancient Lebels, were issued to trusted village militias for self-defence.

H3: SAS nursing sister, 1958 A composite, from two nurses photographed in the Beni-Douala country south of Tizi-Ouzou, where a former para captain had responsibility for 26,000 Berbers in 23 villages spread over more than 80 square kilometres. Travelling between villages escorted by the *maghzen* and men from II/121e RI, this nurse is armed with a 12-bore sporting shotgun; she wears a bush hat, khaki drill shirt, M1947/52 para trousers and *pataugas*, and displays the same green field sign at her shoulder as the troops accompanying her.

Notes sur les planches en couleur

A1 Commando, Commando de Chasse Kimono 36; Ténès, 1959. Un treillis vert ou tenue de camouflage était distribué, avec des calots Bigeard ou des bérets de camouflage. Notez le poignard fabriqué à partir d'une baïonnette allemande Mauser raccourcie. **A2** Moghazni, Sections Administratives Spécialisées; Grande Kabylie, 1958-59. Il porte la chemise kaki M1948, un pantalon vert M1947, des bottes M1917, du matériel de ceinture M1935, le bonnet de police M1946 teint en rouge et est armé d'un fusil 7,5mm à culasse mobile MAS36. **A3** Sergent-chef, 29e Régiment de Tirailleurs oranais, 1959, qui porte le bonnet de police ('calot') M1957 et la chemise de corvée 'légère' M1947. Il porte des sacoches doubles de cartouches pour la carabine US M1 sur la ceinture de cuir française M1946 et sur la crosse de son arme. Il porte aussi des grenades OF37.

B1 Chasseur, 1er Régiment de Chasseurs Parachutistes, 10e Division Parachutiste; Maison-Carrée, Alger, février 1957. Il porte seulement une ceinture sans soutien avec un jeu de sacoches MAT49 et une gamelle. **B2** Lieutenant-colonel Marcel Bigeard, 3e Régiment de Parachutistes Coloniaux, Timimoun, novembre 1957. Il porte le calot Bigeard, un uniforme de camouflage britannique modifié M1942 coupe-vent et un écusson de rang sur la poitrine. **B3** Commando Parachutiste de l'Air, 1957-59. Son matériel sanglé M1950 TAP comporte deux paires de cartouchières M1950/53, le fusil MAS49/56 7,5mm autochargé avec lance-grenade intégré et chargeur détachable de dix cartouches.

C1 Canonnier RCL, infanterie parachutiste, uniforme de campagne d'hiver, 1957-60, manipulant un fusil américain 57mm sans recul et portant le calot Bigeard avec le protège-nuque rabattu, le treillis M1947/52 et /53, le sanglage M1950 et des bottes de para. Il porte un pistolet MAC50 9mm dans un étui en toile M1950. **C2** Soldat, 5e Régiment d'infanterie, uniforme de campagne d'hiver, 1959. Il porte un casque français en acier M1951, le treillis M1947/52 avec poches extérieures sur basques, les bandes molletières en toile M1951 inspirées d'un modèle américain, et des bottes M1945. **C3** Soldat, 81e Bataillon d'Infanterie, uniforme de campagne d'été, 1958. Armé d'un MAS36, il porte le chapeau de safari en toile M1949, la chemise kaki M1948 avec short assorti et des pataugas en toile et caoutchouc.

D1 Soldat de 1ère clase, 2e Bataillon, 152e Régiment d'Infanterie; tenue de sortie d'hiver, Constantine, 1957. Il porte un uniforme en serge M1946 avec les épaulettes de sa branche et le cordon de citation de son régiment. **D2** Soldat, 61e Compagnie de Transmissions, QG 11e Division d'Infanterie; Constantine, automne 1960. L'écusson de la 11e division est porté sur une tenue de camouflage commune à toutes les branches, avec un badge de compagnie en émail piqué sur la poche droite. **D3** Fusilier Marin, 3e Bataillon, 1ère Demi-Brigade de Fusiliers Marins; frontière marocaine, hiver 1958 en treillis M1947 avec l'écusson DBFM sur la manche gauche et le couvre-chef de la marine; une toque de laine; gilet pare-balles américain M1955 et un casque américain M1 portant une ancre peinte en rouge. **D4** Sous-lieutenant, 1ère Compagnie, 2e Régiment de Zouaves; Perrégaux, 1957, qui porte le bonnet de police rouge des Zouaves, une chemise/veste de corvée de camouflage, le pantalon de camouflage coupe-vent britannique M1942 et une cartouchière de cuir SMG simple sur une ceinture à pistolet américain en toile M1936 et il porte un MAT49.

E1 Général de Brigade Jacques Massu, 10e Division Parachutiste; Alger, printemps 1957. Son treillis M1957/56 est modifié, avec une fermeture éclair longue. Sa ceinture de toile M1950 porte une boucle Rapco et il porte des bottes de para marron foncé M1950/53. **E2** Lieutenant de vaisseau, Commando de Montfort; Oran, le 14 juillet 1959. Il porte une chemise kaki foncé marbrée et doublée de blanc. Il porte les épaulettes navales, la fourragère de l'unité dans le jaune et vert de la Médaille Militaire, et toutes ses décorations personnelles. **E3** Sous-lieutenant, Commando Georges (Cdo 135); Saida, 1960. Certains commandos de chasse acquièrent des badges métalliques de poitrine comme le badge en cuivre représentant un croissant et un poignard. **E4:** Soldat, 8e Régiment Parachutiste d'Infanterie de Marine, Tebessa, 1959. Il porte les épaulettes M1946 et le cordon de citation du 8e RPC/RPIMA dans le ruban de la Croix de guerre TOE ('théâtres d'opérations extérieures') sur l'épaule gauche.

F1 Moudjahid, monts Aurès, février 1955. Il porte la calotte berbère rouge et des vêtements civils et est seulement armé d'un fusil de chasse. **F2** Dhabet el-aouel, Wilaya 1, printemps 1958. Il porte un M1A1 Thompson, une arme de prestige parmi les ALN. Il porte la tunique de service de l'armée américaine M1939 et il a roulé un cheche pour en faire un turban de fortune. **F3** Djoundi, bataille des frontières, hiver 1957-58. Il porte un chapeau 'beanie' de l'armée américaine. Sa capote est un modèle distribué à l'armée française et il porte un fusil SMLE Mk III. Il porte une grenade britannique No. 36 dans la sacoche en cuir française ou 'panier boule'.

G1 Djoundi, bataille des frontières, printemps 1958. Ce soldat porte l'uniforme de camouflage version française 'allégée, toutes armes' avec un calot Bigeard fabriqué en tissu de poncho français. A la bandoulière américaine en toile de style britannique il porte des cartouches pour son Mauser K98 de fabrication tchèque **G2** Commando zonal, 1957-58. Ce djoundi porte le treillis M1947, une bandoulière de toile de style britannique avec une gamelle M1951 et des cartouchières de cuir SMG M1946. **G3** Mitrailleur, uniforme de campagne d'hiver, 1957-59. Ce soldat porte un calot de campagne plus épais, en laine, et par-dessus son treillis M1947, pour se tenir chaud, la djellaba nord-africaine.

H1 Lieutenant, SAS. cet officier porte le calot bleu ciel, les épaulettes rouge foncé et un badge sur sa manche, ainsi que les insignes de la SAS (croissant et étoile dorées) avec la manche de chemise kaki M1948. **H2** Caïd berbère, monts Aurès. Il porte un mélange typique de costume local et de vêtements de récupération occidentaux. Le chapeau de paille bigarré était une spécialité de la région. Ses médailles indiquent qu'il s'agit d'un Tirailleur vétéran de l'une ou des deux guerres mondiales. **H3** Infirmière SAS, 1958. Cette infirmière est armée d'un fusil de chasse calibre 12. Elle porte un chapeau de safari, une chemise en coutil kaki, un pantalon de parachutiste M1947/52 et des pataugas. A l'épaule, elle porte le même symbole du champ vert que les troupes qui l'accompagnent.

48

Farbtafeln

A1 Kommando, Commando de Chasse Kimono 36; Ténès, 1959. Es wurden grüne beziehungsweise tarnfarbene Arbeitsanzüge ausgegeben, die mit Bigeard-Mützen beziehungsweise Baretten im Tarnmuster getragen wurden. Man beachte den Dolch, der aus einem abgesägten deutschen Mauser-Bajonett gefertigt wurde. **A2** Moghazni, Sections Administratives Spéciales; Grande Kabylie, 1958-59. Er trägt das khakifarbene Hemd M1948, grüne Hosen M1947, Stiefel M1917, die Gürtelausrüstung M1935, das einfarbig rote bonnet de police M1946 und hat ein 7,5mm Kammerverschlußgewehr MAS36 bei sich. **A3** Sergent-chef, 29e Régiment de Tirailleurs; Oranais, 1959. Er trägt das bonnet de police ('calot') M1957 und das "aufgehellte" Arbeitshemd M1947. An seinem französischen Ledergürtel M1946 und am Kolben seiner Waffe sind Doppelmunitionstaschen für den amerikanischen Karabiner M1 angebracht. Er hat Handgranaten OF37 bei sich.

B1 Chasseur, 1er Régiment de Chasseurs Parachutistes, 10e Division Parachutiste; Maison-Carrée, Alger, Februar 1957. Er ist lediglich mit einem gurtlosen Gürtel mit einem Satz Taschen MAT 49 und einer Feldflasche ausgerüstet. **B2** Oberstleutnant Marcel Bigeard, 3e Régiment de Parachutistes Coloniaux; Timimoun, November 1957. Er trägt die Bigeard-Mütze und einen modifizierten britischen, windfesten Tarnanzug M1942. Auf der Brust ist ein Rangabzeichen angebracht. **B3** Commando Parachutiste de l'Air, 1957-59. Zu seiner TAP-Gurtausrüstung M1950 gehören zwei Paar cartouchières M1950/53, das 7,5mm Selbstladegewehr MAS49/56 mit eingebautem Granatwerfer und abnehmbarem zehn-Runden-Magazin.

C1 RCL-Schütze, Fallschirmspringerinfanterie; Winterfeldzug, 1957-60. Er bedient ein amerikanisches, rückstoßfreies 57mm-Gewehr und trägt die Bigeard-Mütze mit heruntergelassenem, geschlitztem Nackenschutz, den Fallschirmspringeranzug M1947/52 und M1947/53, die Gurtausrüstung M1950 und Springerstiefel. Er hat eine 9mm-Pistole MAC50 in einem Textilhalfter M1950 bei sich. **C2** Soldat, 5e Régiment d'Infanterie; Winterfeldzug, 1959. Er trägt den französischen Stahlhelm M1951, den Arbeitsanzug M1947/52 mit aufgesetzten Schoßtaschen, die Textilgamaschen M1951 nach amerikanischem Vorbild und die Stiefel M1945. **C3** Soldat, 81e Bataillon d'Infanterie; Sommerfeldanzug, 1958. Er ist mit einem MAS36 bewaffnet und trägt die Buschmütze aus Stoff M1949, das khakifarbene Hemd M1948 mit passenden kurzen Hosen sowie pataugas aus Segeltuch und Gummi.

D1 Soldat de 1ère classe, 2e Bataillon, 152e Régiment d'Infanterie; Winterausgehanzug, Constantine, 1957. Er trägt den Kampfanzug in tenue de sortie M1946 aus Wollstoff mit den Schulterklappen seiner Waffengattung und der Ehrenschleife seines Regiments. **D2** Soldat, 61e Compagnie de Transmissions, HQ 11e Division d'Infanterie; Constantine, Herbst 1960. Das Divisionsabzeichen der 11e wird auf dem Tarnanzug M1947 für alle Waffengattungen getragen. Auf der rechten Tasche ist ein emailliertes Kompanieabzeichen angesteckt. **D3** Fusilier Marin, 3e Bataillon, 1er Demi-Brigade de Fusiliers Marins; marokkanische Grenze, Winter 1958. Er trägt den Arbeitsanzug M1947 mit dem Abzeichen der DBFM auf dem linken Ärmel und die Kopfbedeckung der Marine sowie eine Toque aus Wollstoff, amerikanischen Körperschutz M1955 und einen amerikanischen Helm M1, auf dem ein roter Anker aufgetragen ist. **D4** Sous-lieutenant, 1ère Compagnie, 2e Régiment de Zouaves; Perrégaux, 1957. Er trägt das rote bonnet de police der Zuaven, eine "aufgehellte' Arbeitshemdjacke M1947 im Tarnmuster, die britischen windfesten Hosen des Tarnanzugs M1942 und eine einzelne SMG-Patronentasche aus Leder an einem amerikanischen Textilpistolenhalfter M1936. Er hat eine MAT49 bei sich.

E1 Général de Brigade Jacques Massu, 10e Division Parachutiste; Algier, Frühjahr 1957. Sein Arbeitsanzug M1957/56 wurde durch einen Reißverschluß über die ganze Länge des Kittels modifiziert. Seine Textilkoppel M1950 weist die Rapco-Schnalle auf. Er trägt dunkelbraune Springerstiefel M1950/53. **E2** Lieutenant de vaisseau, Commando de Montfort; Oran, 14. Juli 1959. Er trägt ein geflecktes, weiß gefüttertes, dunkles Khaki-Hemd. Sein Aufzug weist die Schulterklappen der Marine auf, die fourragère der Einheit in Gelb und Grün des Médaille Militaire-Bandes sowie sämtliche eigenen Auszeichnungen. **E3** Sous-lieutenant, Commando Georges (Cdo 135); Saida, 1960. Einige commandos de chasse weisen Brustabzeichen aus Metall, wie etwa das Brustabzeichen mit Halbmond und Dolch aus Messing. **E4** Soldat, 8e Régiment Parachutiste d'Infanterie de Marine; Tebessa, 1959. Seine Kleidung weist die Schulterklappen M1946 und die Ehrenschleife des 8e RPC/RPIMa im Band der Croix de Guerre TOE ("für externe Einsatzschauplätze") an der linken Schulter auf.

F1 Moudjahid, Aurès-Gebirge, Februar 1955. Er trägt das rote Berberkäppchen und Zivilkleidung. Er ist lediglich mit einer Schrotflinte bewaffnet. **F2** Dhabet el-aouel, Wilaya 1, Frühjahr 1958. Er hat ein Thompson M1A1 bei sich, was in der ALN als Prestigewaffe galt. Er trägt die Dienstjacke M1939 der amerikanischen Armee. Ein cheche ist zu einem behelfsmäßigen Turban aufgerollt. **F3** Djoundi, Grenzschlacht, Winter 1957-58. Er trägt eine 'beanie'-Mütze der amerikanischen Armee. Der Mantel stammt aus französischen Heeresbeständen, und das hat das Gewehr SMLE Mk.III bei sich. Eine britische Granate Nr. 36 wird im französischen 'boule'-Behälter aus Leder getragen.

G1 Djoundi, Grenzschlacht, Frühjahr 1958. Dieser Soldat trägt die "aufgehellte' französische Tarnuniform für alle Waffengattungen mit einer Bigeard-Mütze aus französischem Poncho-Stoff. Im amerikanischen Textilgewehrgürtel ist Munition für seine Mauser K98 tschechischer Machart untergebracht. **G2** Zonenkommando, 1957-58. Dieser djoundi trägt den Arbeitsanzug M1947, eine Textilkoppel im britischen Stil und hat Feldflasche M1951 und SMG-Patronentaschen M1946 aus Leder bei sich. **G3** Maschinengewehrschütze, Winterfeldanzug, 1957-59. Dieser Soldat trägt eine wärmere Feldmütze aus Wollstoff. Über den Arbeitsanzug M1947 wurde gegen die Kälte die allgegenwärtige nordafrikanische djellaba gezogen.

H1 Leutnant, SAS. Dieser Offizier trägt die himmelblaue Kappe, die dunkelroten Schulterklappen und das Ärmelabzeichen sowie das goldene Halbmond-und-Stern-Abzeichen der SAS und das khakifarbene Hemd M1948. **H2** Berber-Anführer, Aurès-Gebirge. Er trägt eine typische Mischung aus einheimischer Kleidung und abgelegten Kleidungsstücken europäischer Herkunft. Der bunte Strohhut war für die Gegend charakteristisch. Seine Medaillen machen ihn als einen Tirailleur-Veteran aus einem beziehungsweise beiden Weltkriegen erkenntlich. **H3** SAS-Krankenschwester, 1958. Die Krankenschwester ist mit einer 12-Kaliber-Sportschrotflinte bewaffnet. Sie trägt eine Buschmütze, ein khakifarbenes Drillichhemd, Para-Hosen M1947/52 und pataugas. Auf der Schulter trägt sie das gleiche grüne Feldabzeichen wie die Truppen in ihrer Begleitung.